THE WAY IT WAS
Growing Up In the Southwest during the Great Depression

Delma and Walter Runyan

Order this book online at www.trafford.com
or email orders@trafford.com

Most Trafford titles are also available at major online book retailers.

Note for Librarians: A cataloguing record for this book is available from Library
and Archives Canada at www.collectionscanada.ca/amicus/index-e.html

Printed in Victoria, BC, Canada.

ISBN: 978-1-4269-0632-9 (sc)
ISBN: 978-1-4269-0634-3 (e-book)

*Our mission is to efficiently provide the world's finest, most comprehensive
book publishing service, enabling every author to experience success.
To find out how to publish your book, your way, and have it available
worldwide, visit us online at www.trafford.com*

Trafford 12/07/2009

www.trafford.com

North America & international
toll-free: 1 888 232 4444 (USA & Canada)
phone: 250 383 6864 ◆ fax: 812 355 4082

TABLE OF CONTENTS

ACKNOWLEDGMENTS

While most of the happenings described are based on our own remembrances, some of them are based on conversations with our parents, Jerry and Ethel Stoops and Walter and Sallie Runyan; big sister Ethel and her husband John Jeter; little sister Virginia Hudson; our aunts and uncles; our many cousins, particularly Pauline Wiles; and some of our friends and acquaintances. Among the latter are Helen and Kenneth Bean, Alma and Wayne Scott, Ann and Jack Mize, and Clarice and Simon Post. Daughter Kay and son Gregory read various portions of the manuscript and provided helpful comments.

Any picture with no source given is either a family photograph belonging to us, or else a photograph taken by us. All of the sketches were drawn by Delma Runyan, some of which appeared in *Whiffletrees and Goobers by* W.R. Runyan.

PREFACE

For the most part, this is the combined remembrances of the two of us as we were growing up in the Southwest. These remembrances are bolstered by information gleaned from discussions with our families and acquaintances. In order to find logical explanations for some of the things we remember, a variety of references were also consulted, starting with old dictionaries and doctor books that belonged to our parents. In addition, to help younger generation readers better understand the reasons for many of the things that were done then, a moderate amount of history has been woven into the discussion.

I INTRODUCTION

This is not a story of hardship and deprivation, but rather of the manner in which Southwestern inhabitants, both the children and their parents during the very trying times of the Great Depression ($\approx$1929-41), made use of the resources at hand to lead interesting and healthy lives.

Geography has always been an important factor in living conditions and personal experiences. Those of us who lived west of the Mississippi River but east of the Rocky Mountains generally experienced harsher conditions than those found near either coast. The *Southwest*, according to Webster's International Dictionary, second edition, is a rather loosely defined geographic area, but generally encompasses the states of Texas, Oklahoma, New Mexico, Arizona, and parts of Colorado. However, during the Depression Days when we were growing up, we assumed that the Southwest was West Texas, Oklahoma, and perhaps New Mexico. We grew up, respectively, happily sandwiched between an older and a younger sister in a town in the Texas Panhandle, and in rural Oklahoma. Thus, however the Southwest is defined, we think we grew up in the middle of it.

Even though living conditions in the Southwest could be unpleasant at times, what with all of those black widow spiders and rattlesnakes, and droughts and blue northers, both of us thought our childhoods were pretty good. This despite the fact that when looking at some of the pictures taken of one of us in the mid-1920s, based on clothing and surroundings one might conclude that we were about as destitute as could be imagined. However, despite the numerous photographs from that era depicting incomprehensible woe on the faces of the subjects, as we recall, the attitudes of most people were actually quite positive. Defeatism was not nearly as prevalent as some photographers and journalists tried to portray.

The predominant thought seemed to be that if one made careful use of the available resources, survival was quite possible. In general, people seemed to have gone about their normal business. For example, a 1928 letter to the Oklahoma grandmother from one of her sisters in Kansas asked about Grandma's dahlias, when she was likely to come back and visit their parents, and wishing she could be there to help with the wheat threshing, due to start the next week. (The sister did not mean she was hoping for help in the actual threshing, but rather in preparing meals to feed the threshing crew.) One recollection of Mother's that seems typical of the response to what would now be categorized as deprivation involved a visiting brother of hers noticing that one of the well-worn shoes Mother was wearing had a missing shoelace. He said he would fix it, and did by substituting an old piece of baling wire for the missing shoelace. (Baling wire was relatively soft iron wire used to keep individual hay bales from coming apart, and then after the hay was fed, kept for a multitude of home repairs.) The looks of that wire on the old rundown shoe was so humorous, they both burst out laughing.

We both know that despite some discomforts, inconveniences, and lack of social amenities, neither of us starved and that there were plenty of compensations. One example was getting to watch oil well gushers "brought in." Depending on the locale, such things as Indian green corn stomp dances might also be watched and in some locations, arrowheads and fossils could be collected. Our

One of us sitting at the back door of a small two-room house typical of those to be found in the 1920s and 30s on "forty acres and a mule" farms. Such houses had no indoor plumbing, were heated by wood stoves, and had walls only one board thick. Often layers of paper were glued to the inside of the walls with a mixture of flour and water to keep wind and rain from blowing in through the cracks. This particular house was in Eastern Central Oklahoma and was probably built sometime between 1905 and 1915.

parents probably did experience some rather rough spots; however, we think that they too found life quite tolerable.

Oddly, one thing neither of us experienced was the worst of the Dust Bowl days of the 1930s. The Oklahoma native (the older of two brothers) missed the worst of the dust because of the family living just a little east of the driest area, although the little ridges of dust that accumulated on the windowsills and around edges of the outside doors each night are still remembered. The younger brother thinks the dust was pretty bad because he remembers things like walking home from school in the early afternoon and just barely being able to see each side of the road because of the dust. A West Texas brother-in-law, who considers that he did experience some of the worst of the dust, including seeing whole fences buried by it, points out that sometimes <u>sand</u> rather than <u>dust</u> was more descriptive. Depending on soil conditions, the blowing particles might range from fine dust to rather large angular and *sharp* sand. He well remembers his sister's discomfort when caught out in sand-particle storms that played havoc with her bare legs. (People still occasionally report being in a West Texas or New Mexico sandstorm and having paint peeled from their automobiles.) Living in a town, even in the Texas Panhandle, afforded some respite from the dust. Looking at the picture on the next page, however, will explain why a mother commented that during that time she had to dust off her baby each morning. While we three sisters did not require morning dustings, our mother did often give us small dampened towels to breathe through at night. It was also common to stuff rags, often dampened, in cracks around the doors and windows to minimize dust getting into the house. Living in town also generally

A dust storm blowing into Pampa, Texas during the Dust Bowl days of the 1930s. Note that while the cloud is very dense it does not extend very high into the sky

The "Dust Bowl" was rather loosely defined but geographically included the western parts of Texas, Oklahoma, and Kansas. It was caused by a combination of a severe and long lasting drought and farming practices not appropriate for regions of low rainfall.

meant that a family was somewhat insulated from the ravages of severe droughts because family livelihood was generally not dependant on the raising of a good farm crop.

Those of us who lived in small towns in the Texas Panhandle never had the opportunity to catch a subway train or visit a large metropolitan art museum while growing up. An older brother could, however, on warm summer afternoons add more rattlesnake rattles to his collection that he kept in a Calumet baking powder can. It might be added that the avoidance of rattlesnakes became so ingrained in both of us that years later, when vacationing in Northern Canada, we heard something that sounded like rattling, and to the great amusement of the other tourists, took immediate substantial evasive action. The one of us who did not live in town added to his collection of arrowheads. His younger brother found adequate Saturday afternoon amusement, not by attending special children's musical arraignments, but rather by roping goats.

II SPARE-TIME ACTIVITIES

Unfortunately, during the Depression years, "spare time" was not necessarily leisure time! One definition of leisure time is "time free from work or duties." On a farm or ranch the work seemed never ending, so leisure time was either time deliberately taken off (e.g. Sundays) or when inclement weather such as rain and/or cold precluded normal activities. Miserable weather was not necessarily a reason for leisure since there were lots of rainy day or cold weather jobs that demanded attention. Included in these was the repair of harness or saddles, corn shucking and shelling, and during the cold weather, the butchering of hogs. There were also in-house chores involving both rural and urban families that were reserved for cold or rainy days or for evenings if the dim light of a coal oil lamp were adequate. These included shoe repairing, quilt making, knitting, crocheting, tatting, clothes making (old flour sacks were a common source of material), clothes mending, and sock-darning.

Until the wholesale scattering of families that occurred first by the Great Depression of the 1930s and then during and after World War II, most family members lived in the same geographical area. The two of us probably represent the two extremes of what happened to families. While growing up, one of us had a grandmother, three or four aunts and uncles and many cousins all living within a few miles of each other. The parents of the other of us followed oilfield jobs during depression days and wound up a thousand miles from any of their relatives. For the many families who did live close together, nearby relatives usually kept an eye on the children even when

This railroad-style coal oil lantern was originally used by the Missouri, Oklahoma & Gulf Railroad. That railroad was started in 1911 and its name changed to the Kansas, Oklahoma & Gulf Railroad (KO&G) in 1921. The lantern was next used by a grandfather of one of us. Then it hung for some years in a cellar to be available for emergency lighting. Still later, it was carried by a younger brother while coon hunting.

A coal oil lamp much like this one was used by one of us while at home studying his high school lessons.

the mothers had no job outside the home, and aunts and uncles were available when needed as confidants.

Unlike many current doting grandparents, when we were growing up, grandparents tended to put visiting grandchildren to work and keep them occupied with plenty of chores. One cousin's grandparents with several grandchildren had them all visit for two weeks during corn hoeing season. As an incentive to work more quickly, the grandfather placed a small bag with a few pieces of candy at the end of each long row. The children rushed to finish the row, quickly ate the candy, rushed on to the next row of corn and sack of candy, and according to the cousin, productivity increased immensely. Young farm children sometimes played in the fields in sight of their parents who might be doing such things as plowing or hoeing. The mother who as a little girl took her parasol along while she played in the field, once caused quite a commotion while she was "helping" by pulling weeds from the corn her father was cultivating. When she rose up after having bent down to grab a weed, the parasol came up along with her, and rising as it did from a flat field, caused the father's mules to be more than a little upset. By the time her father looked up, she would be bent down again. About the time the mules relaxed and the father was again watching his cultivation, up she would pop. Ultimately, the mules bolted, the father discovered the problem, and the parasol was banned from the field.

Sock-darning, usually considered the mother's and older girls' domain, was rather interesting in that to make the darning easier, some kind of filler was temporarily put in the sock. Those who were lucky enough to have electricity and thus have electric lights might use a light bulb. Otherwise, a small dried gourd or a nest egg might be used. The primary purpose of nest eggs, often made of wood, was not however as a darning aid, but rather they were to put in hens' nests to promote egg laying. The idea being that if a hen saw an egg (real or artificial) already in a nest, she would be more likely to lay one herself.

Clothes making, clothes mending, embroidering, knitting, crocheting, and tatting were also considered the mother and girls' domain, but oddly enough, the father of the three sisters did tatting and also crocheted a large rug every winter. He probably originally took up tatting in his younger and single days for much the same reason sailors used to carve scrimshaw, i.e. to fight boredom and lonesomeness after a hard day's work. (Tatting was lace-like and primarily used as trimming on children's clothing, but it was also used for other cloth edge decorations.) However, his rug crocheting was for the more

Tatting to be used for edging.

practical purpose of providing rugs for the various rooms of the house. Each year the new rug would go into the living room, the one in the living room would go to the next room, and so on until all of the rugs were upgraded and the oldest one scrapped. The children's task was to cut worn-out clothes into strips about an inch wide, attach them end-to-end to make a long-long strip, and then wind it into a ball. Strips were joined, not by sewing, but by cutting a slit near the end of each strip and threading the end of one strip through the slit in the other strip. To make the slit cutting easy, Father made a simple tool

comprised of a board with a razor
blade tip protruding from one end so
that when an end of a strip was pressed
against the blade, a perfectly positioned
slit was made.

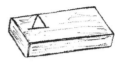

Neither of us ever saw rugs that were made at home
by any method other than crocheting, and we originally
thought just about everyone made them that way. In the
Oklahoma county where one grandmother lived, there
was even a crocheted rug category at the annual County
Fair. That grandmother regularly crocheted small rugs to
be placed by a bed or in front of the living room stove and
also entered one every year in the County Fair. She was
undeniably good and after a few decades of winning first
prize she continued winning as a matter of course. For her
rugs, the cloth strips were joined by sewing the ends
together, usually done by one of the granddaughters.
(Rather than physically joining the ends, it was also
possible to use shorter un-joined strips and just tuck the
ends into adjacent crocheted loops.) It came as a surprise
to us to find that few of our acquaintances from other
parts of the country knew much about crocheting rugs.
One friend from North Carolina did remember his
grandmother crocheting tablecloths, but certainly not
rugs. (Crocheting is still sometimes used as an alternative
to knitting for making various clothing items, and since at
least the mid-1800s, for making delicate lace.)

There were also other means of producing
homemade rugs and apparently none of them were
universally used in the USA, but rather confined to
specific geographical regions. For example, there are two
Oklahoma cousins (but not geographically close by) who
remember that their mother, instead of crocheting, first

braided three cloth strips together to make a wider strip and then with long loose stitches, sewed the wide strips into rugs. This method of rug making was apparently widely used and did not disappear in the 1930s, as is evidenced by an ad of a Chicago company in the April, 1949 *Household* magazine for an "Amazing New Invention" that allowed braided rugs to be made much more quickly and easily then by the usual method. That same year the NU-FLEX CORP was distributing a brochure entitled *How to Braid a Rug in One Day*. The concept is certainly very old, having been used in basket making in ancient Egypt. Upon reading an article by Diana Blake Gray on crocheting and the problems that may be encountered, (www.sandpoint.net), we have a much greater appreciation of Grandmother's handiwork. We can also understand why the aunt, although she did crochet afghans, decided to make braided rugs. A cousin who grew up in West Virginia said her family had a neighbor with a loom who would weave cloth strips into rugs. A recent discussion with personnel at a West Virginia museum revealed that they had no examples of crocheted rugs in their museum, had not heard of them, and thought that all of the homemade rugs made in the early 1900s in that region were woven on home looms.

Store-bought metal needles were used for knitting, a store-bought metal shuttle was used in tatting, but often, for crocheting, the required crochet hook was whittled out of a stick or a sliver of board. One of us remembers whittling a hook for his grandma from a piece of cedar split from an old fence post. Some items of clothing were knitted, but such clothing was easy to snag on things like weeds, barn doors, and tree branches so knitted items seemed to have been more favored by those who lived in cities.

Since there were such a myriad of jobs to keep all ages occupied, rural or urban, there was little time for boredom and not that much time for recreation (leisure time). However, it was generally understood that children needed more sleep than adults and also that they did need extra time for recreation. Unfortunately, because of rural isolation, except at school, church, or during various "socials," for rural families there was little contact with children not in the immediate family. Thus, for those children, except for a few games played at night by coal oil light with their parents, most activities involved only themselves. This semi-isolation also occurred in small towns since the tasks that befell most children of that era did not all get done at the same time, so children from different households were not necessarily available to play at the same time.

Despite these seeming difficulties there were many plain toys and games, and kits that would probably now be called *educational toys*. The later included erector sets, Gilbert's chemistry sets and glass-blowing sets, and wooden toolboxes containing small size carpentry tools such as saws, hammers and planes. Also available were items such as hobbyhorses and kiddy kars for children who could walk but were not yet old enough for tricycles. For children who had outgrown hobbyhorses, stick horses were available. Such horses could be bought but were generally made  by fathers from an old broomstick, a short piece of 2X4

Since so much of the US depended on horsepower in the early part of the twentieth century, as might be expected, many children's toys had a horse motif. Shown above are two examples of wooden horses (hobby horses) designed to be ridden. The top horse was supported by springs so it could gallop, while the bottom one, for smaller children, had rockers for a more sedate ride. Adapted from illustrations in an early 1900s Sears catalog.

A child on a Kiddy Kar. The date of this photograph is not known, but it was probably late 1920s or early 1930s.

lumber for the horse 's head, and some small diameter rope for reins. During the time we were small, stick horse popularity was probably due to the popularity of cowboy movie stars, but some children still like them. A cousin has a picture from the 1990s of her granddaughter riding a stick horse. In fact, stick horses are still available in the twenty-first century from toy stores. The reenactment of cowboy and Indian battles was also a common grade school boy's pastime. Such reenactments required either cap pistol replicas of 45 caliber six-shooters or else homemade pistols (or rifles) shooting rubber bands made from narrow radial sections of old automobile inner tubes.

The brother of the three sisters entertained himself by hunting jackrabbits and rattlesnakes and by building model airplanes and soapbox derby racers (having to build board inclines for the racers since there are few hills in the Texas Panhandle). Along with building model airplanes, many boys aspired to grow up and be airplane pilots (now superseded by the desire to be astronauts), and some, including the older brother, felt strongly that they themselves could fly like a bird. Those who actually tried of course failed and had varying degrees of disastrous results. For example, a seven-year-old playmate climbed a little scrubby persimmon tree and dived off, flapping his arms. He limped most of his life but it was never clear if it was a result of the injuries sustained when he hit the ground. The three sisters' older brother was more innovative but the end result was that he could not fly either. As a thirteen year old, using his model airplane building skills, he actually fashioned a set of wings for himself. He used the lightest weight pieces of lumber he could find for the framework and covered it with pages from the local newspaper. He was then so confident of being able to fly that he announced to the neighborhood the day and time when he would be flying off the east side of the house. There were a fair number of spectators, but our mother refused to watch and said, "He will fly alright, just like a rock." As usual, Mother was right. He crashed, but apparently, the crumpling wings cushioned his fall and thus prevented serious injury.

Nighttime games with parents included checkers, Chinese checkers, dominoes, cribbage, and various card games. The three sisters became quite adept at making checkerboards since in their household, as winter approached, their father would draw lines indicating the squares of a checkerboard on a square end-board from an orange crate and they would then darken alternate squares with a pencil. Meanwhile, for checkers, their mother would sort out black buttons and white buttons from her sewing box. In rural homes, checkers were sometimes made by chopping off sections of corncobs (white corn normally has white cobs and yellow corn normally has red cobs).

Some of the outdoor games played then were much as they are now, but there might be variations from family to family, community to community, and school to school. In some cases, the name then and now may be the same, but the game itself has radically changed. For example, "kick the can," mentioned a little later, was played in the thirties and is still described in game books but the only thing in common is the kicking of a can.

There were also probably more differences between boys' games and girls' games in the 1920s and 30s than there are now, although many indoor activities, such as the playing of checkers, Chinese checkers, and the working of jigsaw puzzles, were shared by both. There were others though, such as jacks, paper dolls, and hopscotch (hopscotch is a game played around the world although different countries do have slightly different hopscotch patterns and rules) that were primarily girls' games. Inside, the three sisters played jacks on the floor. Outside, they played on a slab of concrete that had been a floor to some previous building. Plastic jacks are readily available in stores, and while metal jacks can still be found, in the 1940s, all jacks were metal. Girls could take jacks to school, where playing with them was a favorite pastime during recess.

At home, roller-skating had to be on the outside concrete slab since there were no sidewalks where the three sisters lived, and the streets, rather than being paved, were only dirt, oiled to keep down the dust. Unlike the skates of the latter part of the 20th century, which had both the skates and shoes as integral units, the skates used then were separate from the shoes (regular, everyday shoes). Each skate could be adjusted in length, had a strap to fit around the ankle, and a pair of adjustable clamps to hold onto the shoe sole. Adjustment of the clamps to fit different width shoe soles and to tightly secure the skates to the shoes were made by twisting screws with a *skate key*, which looked much like the keys now used to wind multi-day clocks. To make sure that the key was not lost while skating; it was usually carried on a string looped around one's neck. One Texas friend told us that when he was a boy he recycled old skates by cutting one in two, fastening the two pieces to the ends of a board, adding a few more boards and ending up with a scooter.

Paper dolls were to the 1940s girls what Barbie dolls were to later generations. There were store-bought paper dolls (e.g. Shirley Temple, Betty Grable, Dorothy Lamour), and we three sisters also made paper dolls by drawing and coloring the dolls on cardboard and cutting them out. We then drew and colored paper clothes, leaving tabs to fold over the cardboard doll. When the new Sears catalogs came, the old catalog pictures were made into paper dolls by gluing them to cardboard and cutting them out.

Store-bought dolls of varying degrees of sophistication were common by our time, but dolls continued to be made at home from a wide variety of materials, and in the three sisters' household, such dolls were favored. "Homemade" in the early part of the twentieth century included not only paper dolls and clothespin dolls (described in a later chapter), but rag dolls and dolls made of corn shucks or old socks. The sock doll bodies were made by stuffing socks with something like cotton or old rags. A string was then tied tightly around the stuffed sock at some point to indicate a neck and to define a head. Yarn was added for hair, buttons for eyes, and ink markings to indicate other features such as nose and mouth. Another doll style, more likely to have been found in our parents' time, consisted of a store-bought ceramic, celluloid, or metal doll head and shoulders, and a homemade cloth body. One cousin remembers getting such a doll for Christmas and then not being allowed to play with it because her mother was afraid the ceramic head would get chipped!

It might be noted that though one now tends to think of dolls as having long hair, clothed in fluffy dresses, and being a girl's toy, dictionaries still define them as child's toys. In the 1920s and 30s, small baby dolls were sometimes given to boys two or three years old to play with. In fact, an old Sears, Roebuck catalog lists one doll it says is so well made and durable that it will suffice not only for the first boy it is given to but also for a younger brother. While parents now may have reservations about a boy playing with any kind of doll, a 1930s Sunday school teacher recommended the practice and said it would cause the boy to grow up being gentler with small children. However, it was more common for young boys to have Teddy Bears and indeed one of us did have such a bear, which was a relatively new invention inspired by the earlier president Theodore Roosevelt.

More mundane were the contests to see who had the toughest pecans (this involved putting two pecans, one from each contestant, in someone's hand and letting them squeeze until one of the pecans cracked. The owner of the uncracked pecan got to eat the other one.) Native pecans tended to be smaller, thicker-hulled and harder to crack than the thin-shelled variety, so anyone with native pecans in his pocket, e.g. the one of us who lived in the country, had a distinct advantage.

There were also conventional games such as basketball (in rural schools played outside on a dirt court cleaned of grass at the beginning of each school year), softball, and contests involving marbles, yo-yos, and tops. Playing with marbles, although perhaps less favored by the current generation, dates back to at least Roman times

(1). The rules of the game vary widely with the locale. In the early twentieth century in the United States, most marbles were made of glass, but some were agate, which was favored for marbles used as taws. Taws were the ones used for shooting at other marbles. When steel ball bearings from junked automobiles became available ("steelies") they were sometimes used as taws because they were heavier than glass marbles. Steelies were much more likely to chip other marbles than either glass or agate taws, and in most games were not allowed.

It was widely believed that if a chip were knocked out of an "aggie" (agate) it would grow back in a few months. Of course, such a belief was patently false, but marbles probably did not stay with the same owner long enough for that belief to be checked, and anyway, then as now, eight year olds tended to believe what they were told by other eight year olds, no matter how wild the story. The myth was probably based on the behavior of grindstones, which, like aggies were made of natural stone and which most rural families used to sharpen things like hoes, axes, scythes, and mowing machine sickles. The grindstones, which were about twenty inches in diameter, were primarily made from sandstone chosen to have a minimum of "hard spots." However, in use, any of those little hard spots would not wear as fast as the rest of the stone and thus cause small raised regions on the grinding surface of the stone. When that occurred, it was common to take a chisel, knock out the hard region, and thus leave a shallow depression in the grindstone. During further use, the rest of the wheel would gradually wear down until there was no trace left of the depression. To a small boy's eyes, that could look like the chip had grown out!

The conventional marbles game consisted of drawing a rough circle a few feet in diameter on smooth ground free of grass and weeds and then shooting marbles out of the circle with a taw, with each player keeping the marbles he knocked out of the ring. However, there was another marble game called rolley-holley that was much like croquet except that a marble shooter and marble replaced the croquet mallet and ball, and small holes in the ground in an L pattern replaced the wickets. In this case the prize for winning might be marbles, but it could be anything else mutually agreed on beforehand. Since this game required a dirt surface that could easily be dug in without causing complaints, it was not very common around large-city apartment complexes. (Marbles were called "doogies" in some localities. It is not clear about the origin of the term but one person suggested that it was just boy talk. However, the term was fairly widespread and occasionally used in at least Kansas, Oklahoma and Mississippi.)

One friend, as a boy, was not really very adept at marble shooting, but did like to collect marbles. Having learned how to make kites that flew well, he would trade kites for marbles. The kite building and flying also brought about an early-age lesson  in sorting out what was really the cause of something's behavior. Kites flew well on cold windy days, and after insisting, against his mother's advice, that a particular quiet, cold day would be good for kite flying, found out that it was the *wind* and not the *cold* that led to good kite flying. His kites were made of pieces of well-weathered shingles covered with newspaper so their cost was negligible. The weathering reduced the thickness of the shingle and thus the weight of the pieces split from it.

This same boy would occasionally find and pick up pieces of lead left over from the caulking of city sewer pipe. He also had a few bricks that had stars stamped into their top surface, so he would remelt the lead, pour it into the star depressions, and then stick the upper half of a safety pin into each pool of molten lead. When the lead cooled, solidified, and had been popped out of the brick, there were metal stars that could be pinned to a shirt and make the wearer an instant sheriff.

If a railroad ran nearby, it was common for grade school boys to leave pennies on the track so that a train going by would flatten them into large, thin pieces of copper that could be carried around and used to impress classmates. In towns with streetcars, the streetcars worked, but being lighter, they did not flatten the pennies as much. Coins of greater denomination than a penny were not used for two reasons. First, anything larger really could not be wasted. Secondly, since it was illegal to deface United States currency, the kids assumed that anything as small as a penny would not trigger the wrath of the Government. The wrath possibility was of concern to adults as well, and when silver was needed for decorating things like spurs, Mexican rather than United States coins were flattened and used.

The yo-yo became popular in the United States in the 1920s and has remained popular ever since. It is presumed to have originated in China, was in Greece by 500 B.C., in France by the 1700s, and in England not long after. The Filipinos apparently coined the name yo-yo, and it was a Filipino emigrant who started the first yo-yo company in the United States (2). There were only two variations in the yo-yos that we had. One had the string tied tightly to the axle and the other had the string looped loosely around the axle so that the yo-yo could continue to spin when it reached the end of the string. Now, the tricks that can be done have been greatly expanded by such things as having heavy metal rims and a ball bearing axle sleeve to tie the string around.

There were also some "games" that only required one person. Among these were hoop-rolling and the kicking of rocks or tin cans along the road as one walked to or from school. Parents frowned on the latter activity since it was awfully hard on shoes. (Of course, this activity was never done when one was barefoot.) There was a version of can-kicking (kicking the can, or kicking the bucket) that involved many participants and was usually played during school recess. Despite its name, no mayhem was involved. A circle a few feet in diameter was drawn in the dirt, and the "it" person stayed in the circle with his foot on a can while everyone else hid anywhere on the school grounds except in the school building itself. IT looked around, and anyone he could see was "captured" and placed inside the circle. When all of the obvious people were captured, he then had to leave his can and move away from the circle to look for the other participants. If one of those uncaptured could run up and kick the unattended can out of the circle, everyone in the circle was set free. If, however, IT could dash back and get his foot on the can before it was kicked out of the circle, the would-be kicker was captured and had to stay inside the circle. The game ended either when everyone was captured or when recess was over.

Rolling a hoop required a hoop, e.g. an iron band from the hub of an old wagon wheel. These bands were about eight inches in diameter, light weight, and not to be confused with the much larger and heavier wagon *tires.* Also required was a narrow board such as a lath with a flattened Prince Albert tobacco can nailed to the end of it, and a reasonably smooth road or path. Most smokers rolled their  own cigarettes. Two of the favorite brands of loose tobacco were Prince Albert and Bull Durham. Prince Albert came in flat metal cans that were very well suited for holding fish hooks as well as being flattened. Bull Durham came in small sacks that were good for holding marbles. Hoop-rolling could be a competitive sport when two or more children raced while rolling their hoops. It would soon become apparent to the more astute that the lighter the hoop, the faster it could be rolled. Therefore, those children with plenty of junked wagon parts at home would carefully search for a very light hoop. Misshapen hoops did not perform very well, and one brother tells of the kid who had a hoop with a big weld bead on the outside. There were, of course, no convenient electric grinders that could be used to smooth the hoop so a file, hand-cranked grindstone, or rubbing against a stone were the only alternatives, except that this particular boy never understood the basic difficulty, never tried to remove the bead and thus never won.

Hoop-rolling was not restricted to rural boys even if discarded wagon wheels were the source of the hoops. One boy, who grew up in a small town, raided the blacksmith junk heap for cast-off hoops. He did not use a flattened Prince Albert can on the end of a lath either. He just nailed a short board across the end of the lath. Apparently, hoop rolling was a worldwide children's leisure time occupation, and for example, a 1960s Afghanistan travel book mentions children in Afghanistan towns rolling hoops (3). In their case, however, pictures indicate that the hoops were two feet or so in diameter and were rolled by hand. Despite whatever fun a rolling hoop might have been, hoop snakes rolling along were to be absolutely avoided since they could out-run a child and had a deadly stinger on the end of their tail. A hoop snake could take its tail in its mouth, form itself into a hoop and roll along the ground at tremendous speed.

The stinger at the end of its tail (actually non-poisonous and of horn-like material about an eighth-inch long) was also reputed to be dart-like and to be able to be shot out for a considerable distance. Of course, this whole behavior was the figment of someone's active imagination. Raymond L Ditmars, in his 1939 *North American Snakes* suggested that the origin of the myth laid in the fact that instead of coiling, this particular variety of snake did sometimes form itself into a circle on the ground when resting (4).

When not at school, urban children could play outdoor games with others in the neighborhood. One of those games was Red Rover. For this game, two people were chosen as leaders and then two sides were chosen. One side formed a chain, holding hands. The leader of the other side called out "Red rover, red rover, let Johnny come over." The general game plan (which could vary a bit, depending on the participants) was to call for the smallest or weakest player and that player had to run and try to break through the chain. He would go for the weakest link (the smallest or weakest opposing player). If he were able to break the chain, he could bring a player back to his side, but if he were unsuccessful in breaking the chain, he was captured by the other team. This continued until one side got all the players. Follow the Leader was a game played by both girls and boys. The leader went to the head of the line. The leader could hop, skip, jump over things, etc. Anyone who failed to imitate what the leader did had to drop out of the game. Simon Says was also played by both boys and girls. There are variations of how the game was played, but basically Simon gave directions, i.e., Simon says "Stand on your right foot," Simon says "Put your left hand on your right ear," etc. If Simon gave a direction without first saying "Simon says," anyone who followed the direction was out of the game. Other games included Annie Over, Hide-and-Seek, and May I. Rope-jumping was also very popular, both at home and at school. Generally, only girls jumped individual ropes. Boys sometimes participated when a long rope was used and two players turned the rope while other players would run in and jump. Children sang or said rhymes as they skipped the rope. For example:

> *Mother, Mother I feel sick,*
> *Call for the doctor, call him quick.*
> *In came the doctor, in came the nurse,*
> *In came the lady with the alligator purse.*
> *Out went the doctor, out went the nurse,*
> *Out went the lady with the alligator purse.*

As an alternative to the more standard leisure occupations, we three sisters would sometimes catch large bugs, tie strings around their necks, and hitch them to various little metal road construction toys belonging to our brother. Sometimes small pastures were fenced off with string or thread to hold the bugs when they were not being "worked." Other crawly creatures also provided entertainment in some cases and in other cases provided little entertainment but did prevent boredom. For instance, along with the harnessed bugs, we often had horny toads (horned toads) as pets since they were plentiful in the Texas Panhandle in those days. Unfortunately, horny toads have declined in recent years, and are rarely ever seen.

Old timers who dated back to when the area where the other of us grew up was Indian Territory used to tell how the tarantulas were sometimes so thick they would crawl up the horse's legs when someone was riding through the grass. By the mid-1930s there weren't nearly that many, but killing tarantulas while riding the pastures, and keeping track of the day's tarantula catch by making finger nail marks on the saddle pummel did relieve the monotony of chasing errant cattle. Tarantulas are not really that bad, but to a twelve year old who often walked barefoot through the same area, they could be pretty frightening. However, when a boy did his walking in shoes on city sidewalks, tarantulas were not nearly that scary, and indeed, in later years one of our children had a "pet" tarantula for several months. He put the tarantula in a jar each Sunday and took it to Sunday School, then came home and turned it out beside a hole in the yard where it lived. According to some experts, tarantulas will bite when they perceive danger. However, despite horror stories about how the bite might kill a person, or at the very least, the area near a bite would rot and fall out, the venom is not particularly potent but will cause swelling and some report a pain similar to that of a bee sting.

Ants, particularly the large red variety, will sometimes travel the same path enough to wear away the grass and weeds and leave a narrow but well-defined trail. A rather harmless pastime that one of us engaged in was putting progressively larger pebbles in the ants' path until they could no longer move the pebble out of the path and had to go around. Sometimes normally wild animals could be tamed and became quite satisfactory pets. Usually the animal would be a squirrel or a raccoon, but after we had all grown up, one of the sisters while traveling with her family at night on a lonely West Texas highway, saw two spots of reflected light at the side of the road. There they found a baby bobcat that was sick and had evidently been abandoned by its mother. They took it home, and with the help of their veterinarian, nursed it back to health. It was then raised as if it were a domestic cat. It soon became friends with the family German Shepherd dog, and for some years was a very satisfactory pet and had many traits of ordinary household cats. However, without a prior introduction to friendly humans, full-grown bobcats can, of course, be quite mean and violent. A contemporary tells how he and some of his teenage friends once caught a grown bobcat, put it in an old suitcase and then set the suitcase down by the side of the road. Pretty soon, a car came by, the occupants saw the suitcase, assumed it had something of value in it, and stopped and picked it up. The car then sped off, and presumably, someone shortly opened the suitcase to claim their prize because the car abruptly stopped and all of its occupants came flying out. Domestic animals like goats made decent pets and the brother of the three sisters had one until it got in the house and took a few bites out of some new kitchen curtains. Trying to come into a house was not unusual since most domesticated animals seem to like human companionship. We can, for example, remember the old workhorse that, on summer evenings, liked to stick its head in the kitchen window and watch us eating supper. Another horse, according to our brother, learned to unlatch and open the gate from the pasture to the yard, and then to religiously close it after passing through.

Both boys and girls used homemade stilts. A variation from the conventional design used by the Oklahoma mother when she was small was to get two syrup buckets with lids (one bucket for each foot) of either half-gallon or one-gallon size, tie a string to each bail, put each foot on top of a bucket but under the bail, and by holding the strings, keep the buckets against the bottom of her feet as she walked.

Every boy big enough to open the blade had a pocketknife, and carving initials in handy wood was a favorite pastime. Many a school desk was defaced in this manner, but classmates would then likely chant the old ditty "fools' names and fools' faces are found in public places," and further, if caught, the culprit might be sent out to use the same knife to cut a switch for the teacher to use on him. For these reasons, most boys preferred to do their carving on remote tree trunks. (As a substitute for trees, cactus was sometimes used, particularly the broad leaves of the prickly pear.) Initials in trees could be very long lasting, as for example the ones put by one of us in a big old burr oak tree that lasted over fifty years until the tree fell over. Burr oak has a very thick bark, which is not very conducive to initial-cutting with a pocketknife, but in this particular tree, there were already some initials that had been cut in it many years before with an ax and it was in those big initials that the much smaller initials were carved. More lasting yet, and also more time consuming, were initials cut into stone. Instead of carving more initials in the burr oak, one Sunday afternoon was spent using a hammer and an old railroad spike to chisel name and the date into a sandstone ledge overlooking a small stream. The results of this venture turned out to be quite satisfactory since everything is still quite legible after nearly seventy years.

There was also the game of mumblety-peg (with several spelling variations) that involved flipping a pocketknife with an open blade so that the blade stuck in the ground. In general, the goal was to have the blade stick in the ground in a near-vertical position when thrown from a variety of hand positions (e.g. from the left hand, right hand, back of hand). Sticking the knife blade in the ground did not do anything for the sharpness of the blade so an old knife or one particular blade of a multiblade knife was usually used for this activity. The reason for the concern was that most boys prided themselves on the sharpness of their knife blades and spent much time sharpening them.

Top spinning was wide spread among the boys and most tops were store-bought, but a large empty thread spool was sometimes whittled into a conical shape, and a pencil or sharpened stick stuck through the hole in the spool. (In those days, thread spools were all of wood.) The sharpened end formed a spindle for the spool to spin on while the other end could be twirled between the fingers to start the top spinning. Sometimes the spindles of the heavier store-bought variety were sharpened and during the throwing of the top to the ground to start it spinning, an effort was made to hit and "spike" another player's already spinning top. Tops date back to ancient times and were geographically wide spread. Greek writers, e.g. Aristophanes (ca 450-388 B.C.) and Plato, mentioned them. The Romans made tops from boxwood or terra cotta. In England during Shakespeare's time, a large top was often used for wintertime exercise. In Asia, conch shells, gourds, nuts, and bamboo were all used as material for top-making. Both children and adults have played with tops for centuries in Japan. The Maori of New Zealand made tops from gourds.

Teenagers, while not necessarily liking the games already discussed and not having TV to watch, still had plenty of entertainment opportunities. For example, on Saturday afternoons (normally a time for relaxing in rural communities) it was not uncommon for rural boys to meet in someone's pasture, rope goats and then end up racing their horses. Some teenagers of the era have admitted in later years that after the shovels and other unnecessary accouterments were stripped off, riding cultivators made pretty fair racing chariots. They probably did not hold too well in the curves, but with a pair of tired mules, it did not matter. Going to a rodeo was considered good entertainment, but participating was even better, particularly if one did not mind an occasional broken

A late 1940s small town rodeo during a Fourth of July celebration. Although this picture was taken in the 1940s, such a rodeo had been an annual event there for years. While watching a rodeo provided amusement for the viewers, goat- and calf-roping was a favorite Saturday pastime for many teenagers.

limb. The girls generally only did barrel racing, but with an agile horse,
that could be
pretty scary.

The three
sisters barrel
raced, but no
horses were

involved. In a manner somewhat like lumberjacks rolling logs in a river, they would stand on a barrel (actually an empty oil drum) and roll it along the ground. Two or even three could roll one barrel, but usually there were several barrels available. Racing the barrels was popular with them and many of the neighborhood children. There was usually one favored barrel that rolled smoother and faster, and there was a rush to see who could get to it first. The dishwashing job in the three sisters' family fell to the two older sisters and they drew straws (tooth picks) after the evening meal to see who would wash and who would dry the dishes. When rolling-barrel racing was scheduled after the meal, it was not uncommon for the sister who won the draw to chose washing rather than drying the dishes and then keep several washed knives, forks, and small dishes in the bottom of the dishpan. She could then suddenly pull them out at the end of the job, leaving the other sister to dry them while she rushed out and claimed the best barrel.

Also, while not necessarily condoned by parents, there were things that were sometimes combined with the normal chores or regular farming activities to help with boredom. One could, for example, squirt milk directly into a barn-cat's mouth while milking and simultaneously feed the cat and provide a little break from the milking routine. Then there was the teenager who, when riding a wiggletail cultivator to the field, would sometimes adjust the wheels so that something he had chosen near the path would be run over. The desire to run over things was not, however, restricted to teenage boys riding cultivators. A former classmate, who worked at the White Sands, New Mexico Missile Range just after World War II, said that one of their amusements was to run a Jeep over any appropriately sized cactus they came across. However, one person, fresh to the area, miscalculated, tried to run over a large cactus and found himself in a Jeep with all four wheels off the ground. It was late in the day, and having heard stories about snakes coming out onto the roads at night, decided to spend the night in the Jeep. That was the night the fellow also discovered that even though the desert does get pretty hot in the daytime, it could get uncomfortably cold at night.

Horse-pulling contests were held to determine whose horses were best at pulling heavy loads, but such amusement was more for adults than children. Such contests were usually at county fairs, but we have a picture of such a contest being held between two big teams normally used to haul wagonloads of oil-field equipment. And, speaking of adult entertainment, the father of one of us told how, in a rooming house where he once lived, the roomers would amuse themselves by using a 22-caliber pistol to shoot at cockroaches crawling up the walls. The sequel to that story is that years later, the same father put a 45-caliber slug through a bedroom mirror while practicing his draw. It was not adult entertainment, but in that same house two small brothers spent more than one rainy afternoon picking bird shot (from a shotgun) out of one of the doors. How the

Two teams in a pulling contest in the 1920s. Horse-pulling contests involving pulling heavily loaded sleds were often held at country fairs, but here, two teams on a break from working in an oil field are competing directly against each other.

birdshot got there we never knew, they came with the house.

There were also more genteel means of entertainment. In the very early 1900s, for example, literary clubs were popular. In Wood County, West Virginia where one mother grew up, there were "literaries" (which might have been a precursor to the current Toastmaster Clubs). Groups of young people met on a regular basis where they had organized debates, recitations, or discussions of current events. Both sets of our parents spoke of memories of happy evenings spent with a group of other young people singing, often to the accompaniment of a piano or autoharp. By the time we were growing up, literary clubs and group singing were no longer in vogue. The autoharp was also no longer prevalent, but the piano continued to be popular, at least in the locales where we grew up. For those who could not play the piano very well, player pianos, which were more common in our parents' time than ours, were still to be found. In addition to performing as a regular piano, player pianos could use a long strip of paper with many carefully positioned holes in it to control the hammers used to strike the piano strings. Power to operate the mechanism came from foot-pedal operated bellows built into the base of the piano. The increasing availability of spring-wound phonographs and battery-powered radios were probably the cause of the disappearance of the player piano. French harps (harmonicas) were quite popular among teenage boys while Jew's harps and pieces of paper held behind the teeth of a comb were often used by grade school children to produce some semblance of a tune. Few families could afford an accordion, but occasionally a teen-age girl had one.

In the 1920s, the mother of one of us sitting beside her sister, who was playing an autoharp.

As an adjunct to singing and the playing of musical instruments, in the 1930s when radios began to be more common, the whole family would gather and listen to one for entertainment. However, in our part of the country, there were few stations. There were only two in Oklahoma that this Oklahoma native remembers (Tulsa and Oklahoma City), but there was at least one more because the brother-in-law who grew up in the Texas panhandle remembers listening to one in Elk City, Oklahoma. The first radios were powered by a set of large and expensive batteries (A and B batteries), then a new generation of radios was developed that operated directly from an AC power line. Finally, for those who wanted a radio in their automobile or still had no electric power line, six-volt automobile battery-operated radios became available. When using battery-operated radios, listening was very restricted in order to preserve the battery. One of the programs remembered from the Oklahoma days was The President Roosevelt "Fireside Chats" which we listened to on an AC-powered radio owned by a schoolteacher rooming with Grandmother. (The electrical wiring in Grandmother's house, added after the house had been built with gas plumbing for lights, was certainly not up to current codes in that the individual wires were strung on insulators nailed to the <u>inside</u> walls of her house.) Later, when Father acquired a car-battery operated radio, "Fibber McGee and Molly," "The Grand Ole Opry," "Amos and Andy," and "Bob Wills and His Texas Playboys" were listened to, although being used to going to bed shortly after dark, it was hard to keep awake until the end of a program.

The other of us remembers that when it was time for a favorite program, the family gathered around the radio just as families gather in front of the TV today. The children, i.e. the brother and the three sisters, sat on the floor as close to the radio as possible. Strange though it seems, the remembrance is that everyone looked at the radio as we listened. Our mother was an exception because she took that opportunity to darn socks or do other household tasks while she listened. The sound was often much distorted, particularly when the radio volume was turned up, and the quality was nothing like the high fidelity we are now used to hearing. A station in Clint, Texas (not far from El Paso), was often listened to, but the station call letters or the name of any of the programs simply cannot be remembered. A call to the current Clint station, FM KPAS, revealed that in the 1930s and 40s the Clint station was XELO, with its 150,000-watt transmitter located across the Rio Grande River in Mexico. While not remembering any of the programs listened to on the Clint station, an essay contest sponsored by Cary Salt to describe new and unique uses for table salt, and the many entries submitted in an attempt to win a bicycle or a guitar are still remembered.

It was interesting at night (when reception was best) to see what other stations could be heard. In Eastern Oklahoma, we could sometimes hear WOAI in San Antonio, Texas and KMOX in St Louis, Missouri and almost always the powerful Mexican station XERA. This desire to find more radio stations to listen to combined with the poor sensitivity of early radios and the scarcity of stations led to the use of antennas up to a hundred feet long. Such a long antenna in turn required that there be a lightning arrester between it and the radio in order to protect the radio from lightning striking the antenna.

Even though the radio was initially looked on primarily as a source of entertainment, it also allowed people to have ready access to the correct time. Although by the beginning of the 20th century, virtually every family had a current calendar so the day of the year was usually known accurately, before the radio, the rural population had a problem in knowing the correct time of day. Not only was it difficult to tell whether the cheap alarm clocks usually found in rural households were keeping accurate time, but if a clock were allowed to run down and there was no other clock in the house, resetting it usually involved using a rough estimate based on the position of the sun or some shadow. One of our contemporaries, who grew up in West Texas, remembers that his grandparents would occasionally use a Farmer's almanac to determine the time of sunset for that day in their general geographical area. They would then compare the time of sunset as read by their clock to the one determined from the almanac. This approach is not unlike what was once used in England. Except that there, they watched for the time of high or low tide.

Singing, practiced by the three sisters despite competition from the radio, often caused considerable discomfort to the ears of their parents. They "entertained" the family regularly in the evening with song; so much so in fact that the father sometimes paid

them a nickel each to stop. The repertoire was actually quite extensive, and recently we decided to put together a notebook of the songs sung during childhood. Between the three of us we recalled the titles and words of over a hundred songs.

The childhood preoccupation with smoking also helped fill in some of the young's unsupervised moments. It was well known, even at the beginning of the twentieth century, that tobacco should be avoided. In fact, when we were growing up, cigarettes were often referred to as coffin nails. Thus, most parents, even those who themselves smoked, forbade their children to use tobacco products, though with only partial success. Many preteens tried some sort of smoking experiments. Some of them were quite imaginative, but few actually involved tobacco. A friend recalls lighting one end of a toothpick in the kitchen stove and pretending that he was smoking a cigarette. The three sisters once crawled under the kitchen porch and tried smoking twigs from a dead bush. (One denies it, and when questioned recently, commented "Who do you think told the parents?") In our children's generation, there are candy cigarettes, but in our generation, cigarette fillings of corn silk were common, and sometimes a section of grapevine was used as a complete make-believe cigarette. Our West Texas brother-in-law pointed out that the air paths in a grapevine section allowed hot air to easily reach the mouth, and unless one was careful, there could be a blistered tongue. While not necessarily actually filling them with anything, probably all boys with access to corncobs at sometime made and carried corncob pipes, even though the stems would quite often not even be hollow.

III TRAVEL

On land, for many centuries, goods were transported either on the backs of people or animals, or on animal-pulled vehicles. People either rode on animals (ranging in size from donkeys to elephants) or in animal-pulled vehicles. Horses, mules, sleds, two-wheel carts, four-wheel wagons, and other related four-wheel conveyances have all been used in the United States for the transport of goods and people, and indeed, were all still used during the first part of the twentieth century. Mules were normally considered as draft animals, but a friend's father, who was a mining engineer, spent much of the first half of the twentieth century riding over the mountains of Mexico on a mule. Mules are more sure-footed than horses and he had found out the hard way that mules were less likely than horses to slip and fall on steep, narrow, rocky mountain trails.

We grew up during a period of considerable change in methods of travel and the moving of freight. We saw horse riding be primarily relegated to ranch use, and the buggy become extinct. We saw the automobile become the favored method of travel, the passenger train in its heyday, and the rise of the bus for both intercity and intracity transportation. It was also during this time that trucks began to move substantial amounts of the freight normally carried by railroads, and the beginning of air travel. One of us saw, indeed participated in, the dying gasp of wagon travel. Due to our location, neither of us had any contact with water travel (not even a rowboat). Only when visiting relatives did either of us ever ride a streetcar, and unlike our native New York City friends, who grew up with subways, we never even heard of such a thing. We also had no occasion to travel by sled (although we do have a picture of mail being delivered in the Texas Panhandle by sled), and one of us remembers his father hauling hay on a sled. It is also worth remembering that while one often associates the buckboard with late 1800s travel in the Southwest, an 1899 encyclopedia says that it "was born of necessity in the sparsely settled hilly regions of New England and the Middle States, when money was scarce and roads bad."

Our parents lived through the complete travel transition. Our children though, experienced a very different world. One daughter did have a horse and learn to ride it by the time she was seven or eight, but the other got a motor bike instead. Both were driving automobiles by age sixteen, and by then, both had flown regularly scheduled airlines. Probably neither of them has ever ridden a train.

In our own cases, the "city girl" went through the standard tricycle, bicycle, automobile, bus, train, plane cycle, while the other, in a somewhat different environment, went the horseback, wagon, automobile, bus, train, and plane route, skipping tricycles and bicycles completely. The one who did experience tricycle riding at an early age had it so ingrained in her that she still has dreams of pedaling from Pampa, Texas to Amarillo, Texas on her tricycle with a map clipped to the handlebars! The other of us, who had been riding horses since age six and was never able to master bicycle-riding, finally decided, after a few mishaps, that the problem was likely that his responses to the peculiarities of horseback motion had

A horse-drawn sled being used after a snowstorm in the Texas Panhandle to deliver US mail. The note on this photograph says "U.S. Mail from Canyon to Plainview, March 2, 1903." Those two towns are separated by about sixty miles, and are south of Amarillo, Texas. Photograph courtesy Reeves Photography, Lubbock, Texas.

become so automatic that bicycle-riding motion simply triggered the wrong reactions.

By the late 1920s, in-town wagon travel had virtually disappeared and any rural wagon travel away from one's farm was primarily for things like taking loads of cotton to the gin (usually in the nearest town). However, during the depression days of the 1930s, many rural families were unable to afford any kind of automobile and were forced to go to town in a wagon in order to bring home any large food purchases. Most such trips were made without benefit of the wagon being covered and an untimely rain could play havoc with clothes or a sack of groceries. One of us still remembers our family leaving in a wagon for town with Mother wearing a dress she had just made that had big buttons made by covering cardboard with yellow cloth. With the rain encountered on the trip, the cardboard in the buttons became one unsightly soggy mess. The well-being of the horses during those trips to town also had to be considered, so usually each town had a watering trough for the horses. In the 1990s, our younger brother spotted an old horse-watering trough in an empty lot that we are pretty sure was the one where our father watered his horses in the 1930s.

During this same time, destitute displaced families occasionally used wagon-based living quarters looking somewhat like the cowboy chuck wagon or a sheepherder's wagon, but these served more as homes than transportation. Also, very small farms with only one horse or mule sometimes used a cart instead of a light one-horse wagon since simple carts could be homemade and were much cheaper than wagons. In some sections of the country (not restricted to the Southwest) during the depression years of the 1930s, those homemade carts were often referred to as *Hoover Carts* in "honor" of President Hoover, who was widely believed to have caused the depression.

In established communities, as well as on isolated farms or ranches, buggies were a common mode of travel in the late 1800s and were still in use in rural areas until the 1930s. One reason that buggies coexisted with automobiles so long was because they were sometimes used as an automobile backup and used when the roads were too bad for automobile travel. For example, one of our friends said that as a little girl, her father normally took her to school in an automobile, but that she would be taken in a buggy when the weather was bad and the dirt roads became so muddy that automobiles couldn't travel them. Buggies were used for church going, by doctors visiting their patients, and just for general transportation. The buggy was designed specifically to provide a fast, soft ride. This ride was accomplished by means of a light frame and a set of elliptical-shaped springs fore and aft. That idea was so successful that it apparently provided

An itinerant family of cotton pickers. All but the very smallest children probably helped their parents pick cotton, but likely didn't miss much school because in those days many rural schools (e.g. the one where one of us went) were not in session during cotton picking season. The photograph was apparently taken in West Texas during the depression years of the 1930's. Photograph courtesy the Panhandle-Plains Historical Museum, Canyon, Texas.

the pattern for the Ford Model T suspension when it came along.

One of us remembers an old man who lived miles from town and would go into town every Saturday in his buggy. If he got drunk, someone would put him back in the buggy and head his horse in the direction of home. The horse knew the way and usually took the buggy and its occupant safely back to the barn. One cold, cold evening, however, that did not happen. The buggy turned over and left the dead-drunk man lying on the ground. Our family, who found him, lived in a two-room house and even with the coal oil kitchen stove burning, a butchered hog hanging there never thawed all winter, so they took the man to the barn and buried him under all the hay they had. The next morning, our father saddled a horse and rode over to the man's family, who came and got him in a wagon. The man survived with not even frostbite.

Roads designed for wagons tended to be very difficult for automobiles to navigate during wet weather. It was not unusual, well into the late 1930s, for the dirt road ruts to be so deep that during wet weather an automobile's front bumper would plow up mud. In dry weather, the pounding of the automobile tires produced lots of dust as well as a washboard-like road surface that was very bumpy to drive over. Even though concrete paving was first used in 1865, it was still possible in the late 1930s to travel for miles over a rather bumpy concrete pavement that had been poured in one continuous ribbon with no expansion joints so that it had started breaking up almost immediately. However, even with the many early road shortcomings, the automobile did rather quickly displace horse-powered short distance travel, and intercity bus service became available in the 1920s. The bus bodies were mostly made of wood and used plain window glass since safety glass was not yet available. School buses for transporting rural children were in use about the time as intercity buses and one of us rode such a bus for a short time in the 1930s. This particular bus was not owned by a school district, but rather by an individual, who charged the children who rode it a monthly fee. It too had a wooden body, plain glass windows, and slid a lot on the dirt roads when they were very muddy.

Short distance travel by automobile in the 1930s was not much different from now except that there was no air conditioning, few cars had heaters, and there were no radios or CD players. There were also a few mechanical shortcomings that had to be tolerated. The brakes were just barely adequate for the speeds involved and often failed. A cousin remembers in the late 1920s that as they were going down a long, steep (at least to her) hill, her father realized the car had lost its brakes. To prevent distractions while her father herded the car down the hill, her mother insisted on absolute silence. The low engine power was often insufficient to enable cars to go up particularly steep hills even in low gear. However, since the reverse gear was still lower, sometimes it helped to back up the hill. It was also said that, for some makes of automobiles, because of the placement of the line from the gasoline tank to the engine, if the gasoline level in the tank were low, the gasoline could only flow to the engine if the car were pointed downhill.

Trips of a few hundred miles were, however, a different matter. There was of course, the constant concern of a flat tire since the tires were comparatively

A 1920s vintage intercity bus. From the 1924 United States Department of Agriculture Yearbook. Their caption reads "A Modern Intercity Bus. Comfortable and commodious buses now ply regularly between cities and towns wherever roads are improved, providing a passenger-transportation service which for regularity is not excelled by the railroads."

A family in the mid 1920s ready to begin a
several hundred-mile trip. The whole family
rode in the single seat. To help keep out rain
there were canvas side curtains that could be
snapped in place. The family's entire
belongings were packed in the back.
Photograph courtesy Ruth Brooks of Oklahoma
City, Oklahoma.

The father and grandfather of one of us removing and repairing a tire innertube about 1920. A kit for repairing holes in inner tubes was nearly always carried.

thin and the rubber tread not nearly as tough as it now is. It was not unlikely that there would be some mechanical failure and most people traveled with a substantial number of tools, usually in a large toolbox bolted to a running board. Many major roads were dirt, poorly marked, and occasionally still had gates to be opened and closed.

Most traveling was done at speeds of about forty miles an hour or less, so trips tended to take much more time than they do now. For example, a 600-mile trip on a major United States highway that one of us went on in 1931 took two days and involved camping out one night in a cow pasture. There were few motels (then called tourist courts) and they generally consisted of a row of very small austere one-room cabins separated by just enough space for parking a car.

Despite over seventy years of train history in the United States, traveling by train in the early 1900s was still considered by many to be a very trying and frightening experience, and Grandmother's description of her nerve-racking change at the Kansas City train station is still remembered. Not everyone shared that feeling, and about 1912 the mother of one of us, who was then age 7, and her five-year-old brother were sent on a two-day train trip in care of their twelve-year-old brother. (They all arrived safely at their destination, which was where they were to live since their mother had just died.) Much later, during World War II, the mother of the other of us regularly took herself and her four children on a two thousand mile train trip and never seemed to mind. That trip took three days and two nights and required two changes of trains, one at Kansas City (the same place the grandmother found so frightening), and then at St. Louis.

The trains were generally very crowded, and by passenger accord, any uniformed military personnel were first given seats, then the elderly, and then the women. The non-military adult male passengers took any remaining seats. Children sat in the aisles on suitcases. Sometimes there were dining cars (the meals were very expensive) but for the shorter trips, sandwiches or even a box of fried chicken was sometimes carried aboard the train. Such food was often shared with nearby passengers who had neglected to come prepared. Also, when there were long train stopovers at a station, or where there was a train change, it was usually possible to get a quick meal at a lunch counter somewhere in the station.

The mother mentioned earlier as not minding such a trip did, however, feel plenty of stress associated with packing clothes and food for herself and four obstreperous children. Once, for example, just after arriving at the departing station, that mother glanced down and saw that she was still wearing her house shoes. Since this was in a small Texas Panhandle town, the father had time to rush back home, pick up a pair of comfortable traveling shoes, and make it back to the station. He handed the shoes in through the train window just as the train was pulling out of the station. The difference in outlook between these various people probably had to do with their backgrounds. For example, the grandmother was definitely of the horse era, and she thought nothing of going a few miles on horseback to be present at the birth of one of her grandchildren. The mother with the four children had always traveled by either automobile or train, and later in her life, the mother who was on a train at age seven seemed to make the transition to planes handily enough.

For intermediate distance travel, e.g. between towns not far apart, diesel-powered single railroad coaches (sometimes referred to as "motors") made their appearance in the 1930s and for at least a decade, were used by many instead of buses or automobiles. In fact, at about age 10, one of us would walk two miles to the railroad track, catch a motor to a town about 60 miles away to visit an aunt and uncle, ride back the next day and then walk home. For long distances, conventional train travel remained the preferred method until well after World War II. Wagons, carts, and other horse-drawn vehicles had served civilization adequately for many centuries, but to properly tie together the two coasts of the US, a different kind of transportation was required. Fortunately, the railroad, which itself was many decades in development, became useful about the time it was really needed in the United States. Even though buses had been running between cities since the 1920s, by the 1940s they were not a prime choice for long trips. It might be added that at that time, unlike trains, buses had no restroom facilities. Also, there weren't that many safety requirements for buses and one of us remembers riding shortly after the beginning of World War II in one built in a semi trailer configuration.

The use of airplanes for commercial activities dates back to at least the crop-dusting of the 1920s (5). It was during that time that one of us (about age six) remembers being scared and bending over so he would not be hit as an airplane (the first he had ever seen) flew overhead. The use of airplanes by people traveling gradually gained in popularity, but it was not until after World War II that

A steam engine pulled train moving across the West Texas plains in the 1930s.

travel by regularly scheduled airlines became widespread. In fact, neither of us knows anyone who had even flown in an airplane before World War II.

IV FOOD

Without electrification, perishable food had to be preserved without help of refrigeration. Fortunately, there were/are many other food preservation techniques available, some of which dated back for centuries. Some of the civilizations that developed in regions of no well-defined winter were predominately vegetarians and relied heavily on grains, which were easy to preserve and store. However, the USA was settled predominately by meat-eaters and even in its hotter regions such as the Southwest, those habits did not change. Dried foods such as beans, cornmeal, and wheat flour were, however, certainly an important part of the diet. Even though home canning was used, in general, foods tended to be seasonal. That is, fruit and vegetables were mostly available during the growing season, and meat was either eaten as a small animal was killed, i.e. a chicken, quail, rabbit, or squirrel, or else shortly after large animal butchering, which was done in cold weather.

Electricity was available in towns much earlier than in rural areas, but even where electricity was available, mechanical refrigerators as we know them (called *iceless* refrigerators in the early 1930s) were not widely available in the early part of the 20th century. However, the *icebox*, which in the early part of the twentieth century meant a well-insulated box with provisions for holding a block of ice for cooling was sometimes called a refrigerator and was widely used as ice became available. Before that, boxes with sides of cloth and having the bottom ends dipped in water were used to provide evaporative cooling and were also sometimes called *iceless* refrigerators. When ice did become available from an icehouse in town, blocks of 12.5, 25, 50, or 100 pounds were often delivered door-to-door from a horse-drawn delivery wagon. It was customary for the iceman to carry suitable size blocks into the house and put them in the household icebox. In some neighborhoods, a fixed amount of ice was delivered each time, but in others, a large sign indicating the amount of ice desired was put in a window visible from the street. When ice was picked up at the icehouse by an individual in an automobile, the ice block was carried home on the running board or on a platform attached to the front bumper. The ice was thus kept as cool as possible, and any dripping water was kept out of the car. City icehouses weren't of much help to those who lived in rural areas since the time to transport the ice to a rural residence meant much or all of the ice would have melted by then. However, the ready availability of ice did mean that large iceboxes for storing meat became practical for towns and cities and led to the establishment of meat markets.

Rural foods were much the same from locale to locale but were different from that of most urban dwellers (except for those who lived in very small towns) and were certainly different from those currently found. The lack of electrical power and therefore the lack of refrigeration made the biggest difference, but the lack of a readily accessible grocery store and the general lower level of income all contributed to differences in the eating patterns of rural and urban populations. By the 1930s though, there were a few refrigerator designs that burned coal oil or natural gas rather than using electricity, but they were expensive, rather inefficient, and not widely used.

Since one of us grew up in a poor rural environment and the other in a town of moderate size, we collectively experienced about all of the food storage problems to be described in this chapter. For example, the family of one of us depended partially on small wild animals like squirrels, rabbits, and doves for meat, had eggs fresh from the hen house every day, and drank raw milk while the city inhabitant had meat and eggs from the market and drank pasteurized bottled milk. The general increase in disposable income, cheaper and better transportation, the widespread availability of inexpensive refrigeration, and the trend toward the use of more and more prepared foods has produced widespread differences between foods then and now. These changes have now led to similar eating patterns for rural and urban households.

Because of the problems of keeping meat from spoiling, grocery stores usually did not stock it, but when an ice plant was built in the vicinity and ice became readily available, separate meat markets appeared. By the 1920s, even towns of only a few thousand supported ice plants, and meat markets became common. By the 1930s, some grocery stores sold meat, though sometimes the meat portion of the store was separately owned. As mechanical refrigerators replaced iceboxes, fresh meat sales became an integral part of grocery stores.

Eggs have long been used for food, and before refrigeration became widespread in rural areas, a 1938 *grade school* agricultural textbook was warning that eggs deteriorated quickly after being laid unless properly cared for (6). After gathering, it said the eggs should be kept in a clean room with a temperature between 45° and 65° F. Maintaining that temperature, of course, was not very practical in the Southwest during the summer. Actually, except when shipping eggs to city markets, eggs were usually consumed the day or the day after they were laid. Cooked eggs, either hardboiled or fried, were common items, and it was not uncommon for us to have a cold

An early 20th century general store in the small town of Plainview, in far West Texas. It carried farming implements, many of which are on display in front of the store, food that did not require refrigeration, and some clothing. Photograph courtesy Reeves Photography, Lubbock, Texas.

A 1924 meat market operated by the grandparents of one of us in Kusa, Oklahoma (a boomtown that had disappeared from the map by the 1940s). The building had both gas and electric lights, and while not shown in this photograph, there was also an electric ceiling fan. The cabinet at the back is a large icebox for meat storage.

fried egg sandwich in our school lunchbox.

There was little worry in the first half of the twentieth century about eating fresh raw eggs; salmonella was just not considered in those days. The recipes for chiffon pies all called for raw egg whites, the "best" homemade ice cream had raw eggs in it, and all of us like it or not, probable drank milk with a beaten raw egg in it.

The lack of dependable year-round sources of eggs plus their rapid deterioration led early on to studies of ways to preserve raw eggs, primarily for supplying city dwellers with eggs the year around. A 1928 *Scientific American Cyclopedia of Formulas* devoted over a page to egg preservation (7). The various approaches seemed to have all been directed toward keeping outside contaminants from penetrating the eggshell.

One recipe called for dipping the egg in a water solution of gum Arabic, drying, and packing it in powdered, well-burned charcoal. A "much better" method involved selecting perfectly fresh eggs, putting them, a dozen or so at a time, in a willow basket and immersing them for five seconds in boiling water containing five pounds of brown sugar per gallon of water. The idea being that the boiling water caused a thin layer of hard albumin to form on the inside of the shell while the sugar closed all of the pores in the shell. The cooled and dried eggs were then packed, small end down, in a mixture of a good grade of powdered charcoal and dried bran.

The last method to be developed before refrigeration was probably the use of water glass (sodium silicate) to seal the pores in the eggshell. After coating, it was usual to pack the eggs, small end down, in dry, finely powdered charcoal, or in bran, or in a mixture of the two. There were also some other packing precautions that were recommended. These included starting with absolutely fresh and dry eggs, packing so that the eggs did not touch one another, and minimizing frequent temperature changes. It was reported that the use of water glass combined with proper packing and storage would extend the life of an un-refrigerated egg by months. Even after the widespread availability of refrigeration, work continued on alternative ways of egg preservation. For example, the December 1955 issue of the Farm Journal described the work of a Cornell University professor who devised a process involving removing raw eggs from their shells and encapsulating them in individual plastic containers.

As an aside, dogs as well as people like eggs and in the days when having an egg might mean the difference between breakfast or no breakfast, an egg-eating dog really could not be tolerated. Rather than dispose of the dog, it was the practice to punch a hole in the shell of a raw egg, insert a little ipecac, and place the egg out where the dog would find and eat it. The ipecac would make the dog violently ill (but not life threateningly so), and it did not take many such eggs to break the dog of the habit. Ipecac is a medicinal alkaloid that is obtained from the roots of the shrubby plant *Cephaelis ipecacuanha* and is sometimes used as an emetic (8).

Farmers, and sometimes small-town dwellers, had cows for milk and butter, and chickens (or sometimes ducks, geese, or guineas) for eggs. Farmers with excess cream often churned it to make extra butter, which was then sold, either to neighbors or to a grocery store in the nearest town. To further augment their income, some farmers regularly milked more cows than needed to supply their own milk needs and used a separator to extract the cream, which they then sold. The one of us who grew up on a farm was from the age of ten or so up at five o'clock each morning to help with the milking before going to school. Then, on his way home from school, he brought the cows in from the pasture for evening milking. Sometimes the cream, usually collected until a five or ten-gallon can was filled, was sent by railway express to the nearest creamery (which made butter of the cream) or else it was sold to some local company that then sent it on to a creamery. When the latter was done, the price per pound for the butterfat in the cream was somewhat less than that which would have been received directly from a creamery, but there was no shipping charge and no waiting for payment. In either case, the butterfat content of the cream was determined by a quick test with a Babcock milk tester. One interesting aspect of the cream was that since there was no refrigeration and it might take up to a week to collect a can of cream, the cream was quite sour by the time it was received by the creamery.

Any household that had a cow to supply milk generally also had butter. Cream comes to the top of un-homogenized milk after a few hours and can be skimmed off with a spoon and saved. This is much more practical than using a mechanical separator to do the job if the amount of milk involved is only a quart or so a day. Separators were expensive, time consuming to use, and thus only used when gallons of milk a day needed to be

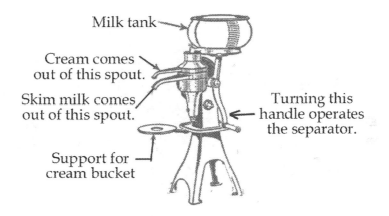

Milk tank

Cream comes
out of this spout.

Skim milk comes
out of this spout.

Turning this
handle operates
the separator.

Support for
cream bucket

Hand-powered milk separator of the 1930s.

If there were more than one bucket of milk to be
separated, two people were required. One turned the
handle and one poured additional milk into the
separator milk tank as required and changed buckets
under the skim milk spout as a bucket filled. After each
use of the separator (twice a day, since cows were
milked morning and evening), the parts that the milk
touched had to be carefully washed and sterilized.
These parts included the milk tank, the cream spout, the
skim milk spout, and the bowl (which rotated at high
speed and contained the parts that actually separated the
cream from the milk). The bowl had to be further taken
apart and had over a dozen parts itself. The separator
was rather hard to turn, so that was Father's task, and
since the washing was akin to household dishwashing,
that task fell to Mother.

A collection point for cream that was used to make butter. The cream was usually stored and shipped in a five or ten gallon galvanized steel can with a tight-fitting lid. The price paid for the cream was based on the  cream's butterfat content. The butterfat content could be quickly determined using a Babcock tester but individual farmers seldom had such a tester. Testing was usually done by the organization buying the cream.

 separated. When enough cream was collected, the cream was churned to produce butter.

   There were small churns holding up to a gallon of cream that had a paddle turned by a hand-operated crank. Larger churns, holding five gallons and agitated by a dasher moved up and down by hand were also available. The one of us whose mother sold butter recalls slushing the churn dasher up and down in just such a churn for long, boring, periods of time. For smaller quantities of cream and a houseful of active children, the cream could be put in a fruit jar and given to the children to shake. (Even though everything from pickles to strawberry jam was put in jars, all jars were commonly called *fruit jars*.)

The three sisters used to dance around the yard shaking the cream to the rhythm of songs and jingles. This is not unlike a method used years before and discussed by Sue Shephard in *Pickled,*  *Potted, and Canned.* (Simon & Schuster, New York, NY, 2000).

   She described a butter-making party in Northern Scotland around 1870 at which "They put cream in the skin of a lamb or the skin of a sheep and threw it from one to the other. By the time it had gone fourteen or fifteen times round the company, you had butter."

   When butter was not available, or when what butter produced was all sold, the cheaper substitute, oleomargarine, could be bought. Oleomargarine, now generally referred to just as margarine, was invented in 1869 by the French chemist Mège-Mouriès and originally used various animal fats mixed with some milk products (9). However, the introduction of hydrogenation to produce a solid fat from vegetable oils led to the elimination of animal fat. The dairy industry opposed margarine, and for many years, margarine was subjected to very restrictive legislation. In the 1930s for example, no coloring was allowed, so that the margarine had an unappealing gray color. To help acceptance of the product, a small package of yellow coloring was included with the margarine so that the user could color it. Originally, mixing was done by stirring in the dye with a spoon or small wooden paddle, but later packaging was such that mixing could be done by kneading the margarine while still in the package.

Hard cheese was also sometimes made at home from excess milk, but based on the remembered results; it was usually not worth the effort. Cottage cheese, which was made from the curds of clabbered milk, allowed any household milk that soured before being used to be put to good use and not wasted. Clabber means the same as curdle, which means to form a curd. Curds are the thick, casein-rich part of well-soured milk. Whey is the watery part of the milk left after the curds are removed. Currently, cottage cheese tends to be quite moist, but it could be (and usually was, at least as made in one of our households) very dry, and to some of us, tasted better. The drier variety also lasted a lot longer without refrigeration, which was very important since there was no refrigeration anyway. Because of this lack of refrigeration, even when there was plenty of milk, ice cream was not generally available unless one lived in town. In the winter, however, when it snowed, snow, milk, sugar, and vanilla extract could be stirred together to give a snow cone like substitute.

Sugar had to be bought, but many people had hives of bees to supply honey and sometimes cane was raised and used to make molasses. Molasses making required a large set of rollers (generally horse-powered) to squeeze the juice from the stalks, and a pan several feet long, heated by a wood (or old cane stalks) fire to boil down and thicken the juice. Uncooked cane juice was sweet and pleasant tasting, so it was not unusual for boys to cut off a piece of stalk (using the pocketknife always carried), remove the tough outer covering, and chew the middle part. Children seem to like to chew things, and as an alternative to cane stalks, if bees were raised, beeswax from honeycombs was a favorite. Yet another alternate, which seems absolutely unthinkable to us, was tar. In the larger towns, tar was used for patching cracks in sidewalks and paved roads, and was thus readily available. A friend, who grew up in a big city and admitted that he had rather liked the tar flavor, also said that when bubble gum became common, those who could afford it switched to the gum. The younger brother said that while he was still going to a small rural grade school, the children had found a barrel of tar (probably left over from roof repairs) in a small school storage shed and that many of them had chewed chunks of the tar.

Both honey and molasses were used directly on wheat bread or corn bread, but either could also be mixed with softened butter to make what we both thought was a very delicious spread. If there were no sugar available, either honey or molasses could be used as a sweetener,

In making molasses, stalks of sweet sorghum cane were trimmed and cut by hand, and the cane juice squeezed from the stalks by running the stalks between a set of heavy iron rollers mounted a few feet off the ground and turned by means of horses hitched to a long arm (sweep) connected to the rollers. The rollers and sweep were mounted high so that there was room enough for the sweep arm to pass over the head of the person feeding the cane into the rollers. A pipe low enough for the horses to step over could be used to carry away the juice, or the juice could be caught in a bucket or barrel and periodically taken to the boiling pan. Several hours of boiling would then convert the juice to molasses. Photograph courtesy the Kansas State Historical Society, Topeka, Kansas.

although some people did not particularly like the flavor of molasses when used that way. In the late 1900s, the health advantages of using honey as a sweetener were being extolled, but that concept was certainly not new. In the 1930s, an elderly next-door neighbor attributed her long life to never having eaten sugar, always using honey instead.

Coffee, like salt and sugar, had to be bought, but there was little attention given to different varieties, although an old Sears catalog did list Peaberry, Mandahling Java, Old Government Java, African Java, Rio, Mocha, and Santos (10). The price per pound varied from variety to variety by nearly a factor of three and probably determined the choice more often than the flavor itself. The making of coffee, now considered an art by some coffee drinkers, as practiced by some consisted of pouring ground coffee into a pot of water and boiling the daylights out of it. Any coffee remaining from breakfast was often just left in the pot, along with the grounds, and drank later in the day. However, other households felt differently. For instance, a brother-in-law from the Texas Panhandle recalls that in the 1930s, his grandparents still bought their coffee beans in bulk, unroasted and unground. They then roasted them in a skillet, shaking them and watching them until they were deemed "done." The beans were then ground in a small hand grinder and used immediately. He also remembers the discussions the grandparents would have after each roasting about what changes needed to be made the next time. Whether they bought the raw beans and roasted them themselves because that was all that was readily available where they lived or whether they were true coffee aficionados is not known.

While vacuum-packed ground coffee in metal cans (to preserve flavor after grinding) became available in the 1920s, and with modifications is still used, it was expensive (11). During World War II, because of metal shortages, glass jars were sometimes used, and in the twenty-first century, plastics technology has improved enough for plastic containers sometimes to be used. In the early 1920s, roasted coffee in bulk was bought by small stores and then weighed and ground in large hand-powered grinders to customer specifications of fine, coarse, or in between. By the 1930s, most people bought roasted whole coffee beans in one-pound sacks, and had them ground at the store and repackaged in the same sack (by then the stores used electrical power). Of course, since the end of the twentieth century, roasted whole coffee beans in one-pound sacks can again be bought, the only difference being that while the stores provide the grinders, the customers themselves grind and repackage the coffee in the same sack.

Where there was enough rainfall, gardens provided vegetables during the summer months and if the excess were canned or otherwise saved, during the winter months as well. The varieties of vegetables grown then were not much different from those grown now. Potatoes and onions could usually be stored for several months if kept dry and any rotten ones periodically removed (a smelly job usually reserved for the children). The onions were tied in bunches and hung on the wall or from rafters, and the potatoes stored in a cool place, such as under the house or in a cellar if there was one. Cellars or basements intended for storage purposes were most likely to be found in the Northern part of the USA, but

Wooden box home coffee grinder. The coffee being ground had often been roasted just minutes before in a skillet on the kitchen stove. The roasted beans were poured into the grinder hopper and the ground coffee caught in the small drawer. The design dates back to the 1800s but this kind of grinder was still being used in some rural homes in the 1930s.

Hand-operated grocery store coffee grinder. This particular machine was used in a store in a small town in Oklahoma in the 1920s. Usually a pound at a time was ground. In the 1930s it was used to grind corn for feeding milk cows.

since much of the Southwest was very prone to tornadoes, many rural and small-town houses had cellars close by.

A non-food plant sometimes grown in small quantities if the climate was right was tobacco. A neighboring farmer who could not afford to buy sacks of Bull Durham or cans of Prince Albert (the most popular brands of tobacco, at least in our region) raised a few plants each year and "cured" them by hanging them on a barbed wire fence. What he used for cigarette paper we cannot recall. (Remember that in those days most people who smoked cigarettes hand-rolled their own although both small portable cigarette rolling machines and store-bought cigarettes were available.) Incidentally, even though at the beginning of the twenty-first century some people continued to say that no one ever told them of the health hazards of smoking, the 1902 Sears, Roebuck Catalogue advertised "A Sure Cure for the Tobacco Habit" and commented that "Nicotine is a virulent poison and the chief ingredient of tobacco."

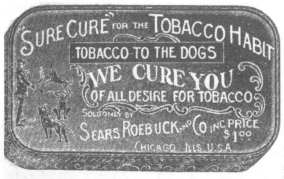

WE CURE YOU This is nature's own remedy, entirely harmless. It cures because it builds up and fortifies, rejuvenates the weak and unstrung nerves caused by over indulgence in this poisonous weed. It stops the craving for tobacco by supplying instead a healthy nerve tonic and strengthener; it does more, it eradicates the poisonous nicotine from the system which has accumulated from long continued use of tobacco. Nicotine is a virulent poison and the chief ingredient of tobacco.

Things like cucumbers, as well as some other vegetables and various fruits (e.g. peaches) that could be preserved by salt or vinegar were often not canned, but rather pickled. The term "pickling," while sometimes applied to preserving in brine, usually referred to preservation in vinegar solutions, although fruit pickling solutions were usually a vinegar-sugar mixture. Fermentation has also been used as a means of preservation and as a flavor enhancer, with sauerkraut probably being the best known. One of us remembers our mother making the kraut in five-gallon crocks. Food preservation by fermentation was not only used for food consumed by humans but also occasionally for food eaten by livestock. As an example, the silos that were at one time so much a part of the American rural scene were built to store and promote the fermentation of the fodder they contained.

Dried beans were easily stored, and were a staple of winter food for many families. Natural drying has been used for preserving things like beans, wheat, barley, rye, millet, and rice since their introduction into the food chain. Kept in a dry place, such grain will remain edible for centuries, as has been observed with beans found in cliff dwelling remains. Grass, preserved by drying (hay) has long been used for feeding domestic grass-eating animals, and it has been reported that the desert rodent Pika cuts grass with its teeth, dries it, and stores it for later use as food (Smithsonian, March, 2006). Most grain was used to make bread, and as a natural extension, drying was also applied to the bread. The result was a variety of dried breads that were very hard, would keep for months, and needed to be soaked in some liquid before eating.

Many fruits have also been preserved by drying. In hot dry climates, grapes, figs, and dates were dried by leaving them in the sun. In damper regions such as England, apples, pears, and plums have been dried in ovens since the middle ages. Drying has also been used to preserve peppers and some herbs. Meat can be preserved by drying alone but often drying was used in conjunction with salting or smoking. There is evidence that drying was used for fish and poultry many centuries B.C. It should be remembered that dryness does not necessarily imply a hot climate and it was in the cold Northern regions, where during the cold winters the air can be quite dry, that the preserving of fish by drying was developed quite early.

In some regions, black walnuts, hickory nuts, and pecans were gathered in the fall and would keep for at least a year before becoming rancid. They were not considered as serious food, but rather more like "snacks" or for use in pies, cakes and candy. In most parts of the United States, it was not the thin-shelled English walnuts that were saved, but the very thick-shelled, hard-to-crack native black walnuts. The more expensive English walnuts (mostly from California) were generally available as a treat at Christmas, but many of us liked the harder-to-shell black walnuts much better. While the thin-shelled English nuts were easy to shell, to effectively crack a black walnut required a large hammer and something heavy, like a sledgehammer or a large rock, to put the walnut on. Pecan shells are generally thin enough that anyone with a good grip can put two of them side-by-side in their hand and crack one of them.

Where there were oak trees, acorns could be collected, and with proper treatment, be used for food. Acorns' high tannin content makes them unfit for human consumption unless the tannin is removed, but the Indians ground them, soaked them in water to remove the tannin, and then ate the resulting mush (12). Ranchers and farmers, however, apparently never considered acorns very seriously as a food, perhaps because they shared the view of one early traveler who asserted that the taste, while not very pleasing, was not positively disagreeable. While corn was widely grown in the Southwest, wheat was not, so in that section of the United States, wheat flour, like salt, sugar, and coffee, always had to be bought, but cornmeal, ground from homegrown corn, was produced locally. By the 1930s there were mills (often hammer mills driven by engines from old Model T Fords) locally available to do the grinding. Of course, just about anywhere that corn was grown; roasting ears were eaten in season.

A few wild plants were also eaten. Sheep's sorrel (probably wood sorrel) was often picked and chewed raw for the flavor. For those who liked cooked greens, and some of us did not and do not, salad of wild poke (pokeweed, *Phytolacca americana*) was considered quite a delicacy. The leaves of poke were, and are, thought to be poisonous so they were never eaten raw but were boiled in a series of waters to leach out the poison. There have been a few letters to the editor in local newspapers that have proclaimed the leaves not to be poisonous and an encyclopedia just says the roots are poisonous, but we know of no one who ate the cooked greens without changing the water a few times. The undried seeds are filled with a red liquid that has sometimes been used as a dye. The possibility that some of the wild-growing plants might be harmful was not taken lightly, but one housewife did forget and cooked a pot full of wild carrot tops (probably not the right name, but that is what we called them) for her husband. The result was that he was completely out of his mind for a few hours. Not knowing

The mother of one of us picking roasting ears (immature ears of corn) from an Oklahoma cornfield in the 1930s. Since the stalks were so high, the corn was probably field corn and not the *sweet corn* normally raised for roasting ears. This corn was growing in a very fertile creek bottom, and like the song in Roger's and Hammerstein's OKLAHOMA, was "as high as an elephant's eye."

if the man might become violent, one of the neighbors stood by with a lariat rope to catch and tie him if necessary (which it wasn't), and the next morning the effects had worn off.

There were often fruit trees about, particularly apple and peach, so even in the backyards of small town dwellers, some fresh fruit might be available as it ripened. In addition to being eaten fresh, some of the fruit was canned, and some used for making jelly. Because of its high sugar content, jelly would last for a long time without being sealed, although it might mold on the surface. The mold was, of course, scraped off before the jelly was eaten. Besides the orchard-type fruits there were wild fruits such as mulberries (smaller fruit than the domestic variety), possum grapes, persimmons, and the fruit of the prickly pear cactus that could be eaten, although most of them required that some precautions be taken. Unwashed (the way we normally ate such things), the tiny bugs and worms in the mulberries were particularly bad. The possum grapes were rather benign, consisting primarily of skin and seeds. Some of us liked them though, and one of us would gather up a gunnysack of them and convince Mother to boil them down and make juice. (Gunnysacks were made of jute and designed to hold 100# of livestock feed.)

If persimmons are not quite ripe they are <u>very</u> astringent so that biting into a green one is somewhat like taking a mouthful of alum. Dogs, coyotes, and horses all seem to be impervious to the high content of tannin in the green persimmons and dearly love ripe ones. There was an old horse that would even go up to a persimmon tree, put his shoulder to it, and shake down persimmons. This was not unlike the story in a grade school reader about the ox who broke open pumpkins by pressing down on them with his head. Prickly pears have a little cluster of fine needles at the end of each pear, which certainly need to be removed before eating. One of us removed far more than his share by the simple expedient of stubbing his bare foot (when going barefooted through the pastures) against the cactus and transferring the needles to his toe.

There were also small peaches to be found, usually around old house sites, that were referred to as "Indian" or "native" peaches. A Dallas, Texas horticulturist said in a question and answer column that there is no such thing as a "native" peach and that he never heard of an "Indian" peach. (Peaches are not indigenous to North America.) Probably what was observed were trees that grew up from the rootstock after the grafted portion had died from lack of water. (There is a similar tree in our backyard now.)

Before the widespread use of refrigeration, most meat was not preserved, but rather butchered and eaten before spoiling could occur. Cool winter months provided natural refrigeration so that large animals such as hogs and cattle could be butchered and consumed before spoilage occurred. While hog butchering was often done entirely by individual families, it was sometimes more of a social event, with neighbors bringing food, and then helping to cut up the meat and grind the sausage. In return, the neighbors would likely take home some of the freshly made sausage or the makings of some headcheese. A heifer or steer is larger than a hog, requires skinning, and in general is considerably harder to butcher than a hog, so by the 20th century cattle were generally butchered in slaughterhouses.

In warm months, small animals that could be eaten before spoiling were necessary unless much waste could be tolerated. Thus, small wildlife such as birds (e.g. quail and doves), rabbits, and squirrels were hunted during those months. Medium-size domesticated animals such as sheep, goats, and pigs could also be economically used in warm months by large families or social gatherings. Normally though, small domesticated animals such as chickens, guineas, and ducks, along with salt-cured bacon, were the fare during summer. After several months of eating nothing but chicken over sixty years ago, the thought still is that one needs to be awfully hungry before again considering chicken. When none of these was available, there were sometimes substitutions, often not very palatable. One of us, for example, has eaten blackbirds (it takes a lot of them) and opossum (very greasy). Large city apartment dwellers with access to rooftops also sometimes kept pigeons for eating. The young pigeons (squabs) were considered by many to be quite a delicacy. It should be mentioned that a friend who grew up in New York City remembers there having been pigeon houses (dovecotes), but thinks that the pigeons were only used for racing.

Canning of fruit and vegetables was becoming common by the end of the nineteenth century. Canning was developed by Nicolas Appert of France who had successfully demonstrated the preservation of both meat and vegetables in glass bottles by 1803. In 1910, P. Durand of England patented the use of metal cans, which are now used for almost all commercial canning. Canned fruits, vegetables, and meats in metal cans were available in grocery stores throughout most of the twentieth century. There wasn't much choice of meats, but corned beef and sardines were both well-liked. During the winter months canned goods could be used to supplant the homegrown diet if a store was within reach and money could be found. Also, home canning was very popular, particularly in rural homes, with glass jars having thin metal lids sealed by thin rubber gaskets being used. Fruits and vegetables were the items most often canned, but occasionally meat was also canned. The successful home canning of meat was difficult and in general, at least as we remember it, the results were not particularly tasty. A friend though does remember how good some of her mother's canned pork was. Pickling was complex and many people did not like the taste of pickled meat. Drying was only applicable to thin strips, e.g. beef jerky, and was seldom used. That left smoking and salting as the common preservation methods. Salting was/is a time-honored way of curing and preserving meat and has also sometimes been used to preserve fruits and vegetables. There were/are two ways of salting: wet or dry. The wet method immersed the meat in a brine consisting of a solution of common salt in water. In the dry method, salt was rubbed on the meat and then generally the meat was packed in more salt. One example of meat preserved by salting is corned beef, with the name coming from the English use of the term "corn" to describe the salt granules used in the preservation. Smoking, usually proceeded by some form of salting, could be used for preservation and was sometimes preferred because of the taste imparted.

Hams, bacon, and salmon were three items usually smoked. There are two modes of smoking: cold smoking, which does not cook the meat at all, and hot smoking, which does partially cook it. Before the introduction of the modern small smokers, smoking was done in specially designed rooms or "smokehouses." Smoking did not seem to be used in the Southwest, primarily because the weather could not be depended on to remain cold enough to keep the meat from spoiling during the time it took to properly smoke it. There was also a liquid smoke available that the meat could be soaked in, but did not seem to have been very popular.

A *sugar-cure* was also sometimes used for preserving hams. Originally, the sugar-cure was mixed according to family recipes, but by the 1930s, it could also be bought commercially, as for example, Morton's Sugar-Cure. Salting required that the meat be kept well covered with salt and worked best with thinner cuts such as sides of bacon. Occasionally, some different preservation method would be tried, often with unexpected and sometimes disastrous results. A brother-in-law remembers that one fall they packed some pork shoulders and hams in a small barrel and then filled the barrel with linseed oil. When the barrel was opened some months later, after the oil was cleaned away the pork looked and tasted all right but the odor was so bad they never tried that method again. There were some dishes prepared fresh in conjunction with butchering that were not for the squeamish. One, looked on with longing by one of our mothers as long as she lived was headcheese. According to an old cookbook (13) headcheese was made as follows: Select a hog's head and wash thoroughly; simmer for 4 hours in water to which some vinegar has been added; remove meat from bones and grind all lean meat, tongue, brains, and skin; add salt, pepper, sage, savory, basil, marjoram; pack in a mold, chill, and slice. In anticipation of such a use, the hair would have been removed from the head during butchering. Actually, the concoction tastes as bad as it sounds.

When butchering, excess fat cut from the carcass was always saved. That from cattle and sheep was/is called "tallow," and not being very flavorful, was seldom used for cooking. In the generation before us, much of the tallow was used for making soap, and before that, for making candles. (One of us remembers his grandmother making lye soap, and the other remembers her mother making one batch of soap so the three sisters could see how it was done.) Tallow, along with neat's-foot oil, was also used in making a preparation for keeping harness leather from cracking. (*Neat* refers to bovines, and neat's-foot oil is obtained by boiling the shinbones and feet of cattle.)

Hog fat (lard) was widely used in cooking, particularly for frying, and for flavoring. For example, what we both thought was one of the very best summer salads involved pouring hot bacon grease over greens to "wilt" them. This is an example of the food now included in the "if it tastes good spit it out" list! Much of the lard was rendered (rendering is to extract by melting, in this case fat from tissue) from scraps cut from the carcass while it was being cut up into smaller, standard pieces for such things as ham, bacon, spare ribs, and pork chops. Often the scraps would be skin and a little fat. The pieces of fried pork skin remaining after rendering were called cracklings, and were often chewed like gum. Cracklings should not be confused with chitlings (chitlins, chitterlings) which were/are fried sections of hog intestines. Chitlings were not often eaten in the Southwest; they seemed to have been more of a Southern dish. Tripe is somewhat related, with plain tripe being composed of the walls of the paunch of a ruminant, e.g. a cow, and honeycomb tripe being the walls of the reticulum (second stomach). Neither of us remembers ever encountering tripe in the United States, but has seen it in restaurants in Mexico where it is called *menduo*. Fat from chickens was also sometimes rendered and saved. A friend from New York remembers how good bits of chicken skin and sliced onion were when cooked in that chicken fat.

Organ meat was eaten, partly because of its pronounced flavor, but also because of the desire not to waste any edible part of the butchered animal. Scrambled eggs and brains was a much-favored delicacy by our fathers, and one of us always thought that cooked beef heart, when stuffed with dressing and sliced thinly, was not only very good but also very pretty. Fried chicken livers were also liked very much. Beef tongue could be boiled and sliced for sandwiches. It was not very good, and while cooking, the disagreeable odor could be smelled all the way to the barn. The use of organ meat and other cuts that seem unsavory to us now was not peculiar to the Southwest, or indeed to the United States. We have, e.g., an old travel book that describes how the 1850s Arctic explorers relished raw polar bear liver. We also have a 1950s Mediterranean cookbook (14) that comments "--the butcher's stalls are festooned with every imaginable portion of the inside of every edible animal (anyone who has lived long in Greece will be familiar with the sound of air gruesomely whistling through sheep's lungs frying in oil)."

There was also the belief held by many well into the 1940s, that organ meats were particularly good for a person. For example, the same 1947 cookbook with the headcheese recipe says "The meats most important nutritionally are liver, kidney, brain, spleen (milt), thymus (sweetbreads), and heart. --- The function of these meats in the living animal is to carry on vital life processes; therefore they contain proteins of the most superior quality and larger quantities of many vitamins and minerals than do muscle meats." Such beliefs are now in disrepute, and fortunately, the ready availability of refrigeration and a good transportation system makes it possible to obtain wholesome meat anywhere in the United States. Refrigeration as a means of extending the life of fresh meat began to have an impact early in the twentieth century, although ice harvested and stored in the winter had been used in the Northern States for several decades previously to keep meats cool. By the 1930s, Birdseye had developed a quick freeze method of supplying frozen foods (mostly vegetables) that were palatable when thawed, but such foods did not become popular until the last half of the twentieth century.

With regard to alcoholic drink, its home production was seldom openly advertised since such activity was generally illegal, but it was certainly carried on. This activity could (and can) be broken into the two categories of high alcohol content distilled liquor and weaker beer-like beverages. Distillation was more involved, the still was generally outdoors, and there was usually some evidence of activity, as for example, the tipsy hogs that showed up from time to time. In Oklahoma, our hogs were often allowed to roam unfenced, and periodically some of them would break into a vat of mash and show up at night somewhat inebriated. It was also not uncommon for one neighbor to help another carry a still to a creek or pond and temporarily sink it when word came of an impending sheriff's visit. The pervasiveness of local distillation was also demonstrated by the fact that in the nearby town where one of us attended high school it was understood that any brand of whisky one might want was inexpensively available at an old rundown hotel by the railroad tracks. It was only necessary that an empty bottle could be found with the desired label on it. The weaker, non-distilled liquor, often referred to as "home brew" could vary from being carefully made from good ingredients to the 1930s depression days approach of using any ingredients cheaply available that would ferment, was drinkable, and as one old-timer said, "gave a buzz." In some locales, e.g. Oklahoma, such drinks were often called choc beer with the original recipe presumed to have originated in the Choctaw Nation of Indian Territory sometime before Oklahoma became a state. One of the more conventional Depression Days recipes used whatever fruit was in season, a handful of raisins, yeast, malt, and sugar. Another cheaper and more common approach used over-ripe fruit discarded by grocery stores. The fruit, some yeast, and water was just put in a bucket and shoved under the porch (in summer) for a few days. Even further down the quality scale, the fermented ensilage juice that collected in the bottom of vertical silos was sometimes drank.

Cooking The actual food prepared varied with the season and from place to place, but grease was widely used for seasoning and it was also not uncommon to drop slices of bread into the hot skillet of grease remaining after frying bacon and brown them as they soaked up the bacon grease. The father of one of us often did that. Everyone knew that animals for butchering should be fat, but an 1884 farm manual emphasizes the fact with the statement: "The lamb should be young, and of course fat; a lean lamb is not worth killing." That same manual suggests that no table is complete without a variety of sauces, but salt and pepper is about all we ever saw.

Cooking was mostly done on either wood- or coal-burning stoves, although in some regions there was a gas supply and gas cook stoves were used. A large wood- or coal-burning cook stove produced a substantial amount of heat, and in fact, might keep an entire small house warm when the weather was not too cold. During the summer, cooking a large meal on such a stove could be quite uncomfortable. To solve that problem, one acquaintance said her family had a coal oil stove for summer use. The only time the wood stove was used in the summer was when something large, like a turkey, was roasted. The coal oil stove did not need to be connected to a chimney and was left setting in the kitchen the year-round.

There was no good way of judging the temperature of ovens, pans or skillets, and certainly no automatic temperature control. Thus, pie- and cake-baking was an art, and any individual who could bake a superior angel food cake was held in high esteem. One grandmother, along with one aunt, were the angel food experts. A cousin remembers that the aunt always used thirteen egg whites in her cake, and the three sisters remember that their mother also used thirteen. The recipes of the day mostly specified ten or twelve egg whites, so maybe the extra egg was the secret of a really good cake. That grandmother's green grape pie was also very good! Mother and the other aunts were OK for baking most other pies and simple cakes. To get some idea of whether or not a skillet was at cooking temperature, it was not uncommon to stick a finger in one's mouth and then touch the skillet and listen to the amount of sizzle. To check an oven to see if its temperature was right for baking, some would open the oven door and momentarily stick their hand inside. This approach was not unlike the sticking of one's hand and arm out a door in the wintertime to get an idea of how big a coat to wear.

To vary the temperature of the oven or stovetop of a wood- or coal-burning stove there were several controls available. The first was just to vary the size of the fire by the amount of coal or wood put in the firebox. By removing a stove lid and setting the utensil to be heated over the open hole to the firebox below, maximum heating was obtained. At least one stove lid was generally made up of a graduated nest of two or three flat  cast iron rings so that the size of the hole open to the firebox could be adjusted by choosing the number of rings removed. If removing the whole lid provided too much heat, then a smaller hole could be chosen. There were also a series of dampers to control the speed of burning by adjusting the air intake. The stovepipe usually had a damper somewhere between the stove and the chimney. The stove itself had one or more adjustable air inlets to the firebox. Thus, controlling the stove temperature required quite a number of adjustments. Along with temperature, bread- and cake-baking also required that the oven not be shaken so that the risen dough would not fall and leave the cook with a flat cake or loaf of bread. Thus, oven doors had to either not be opened at all or else be very carefully opened and closed. Further, because the floors of most houses were rather poorly supported and given to

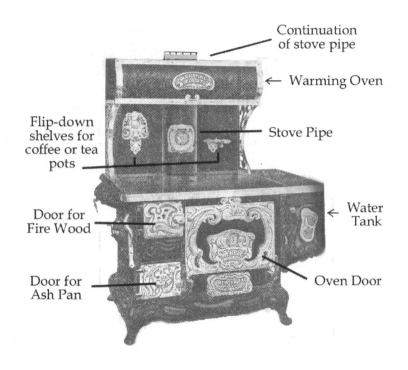

Continuation of stove pipe

← Warming Oven

Flip-down shelves for coffee or tea pots

Stove Pipe

Door for Fire Wood

← Water Tank

Door for Ash Pan

Oven Door

Wood or coal kitchen stoves varied from small and plain ones to very ornate models like the one above. The rural mother had one much like this one except that it was very old. The warming oven was heated by the hot smoke in the stove pipe, which went up through the warming oven. The optional water tank held several gallons of water, and was heated from the fire in the stove. (Adapted from an old Sears Roebuck catalog illustration.)

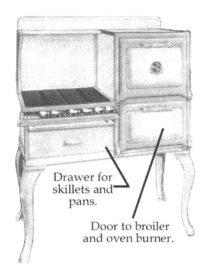

Drawer for
skillets and
pans.

Door to broiler
and oven burner.

By the 1930s, gas stoves were constructed without the heavy cast iron components of wood and coal stoves and were thus able to take advantage of the rapid heating and cooling possible with gas burners. Such stoves were, however, not able to heat a kitchen on a cold winter day like a wood stove could. On the other hand, they were much more comfortable to be around in the summer. The grandmother of one of us had a stove like this one.

shaking when walked across, running children were usually banned from the kitchen during baking sessions.

Although it may be a bit surprising, ovens could, and sometimes were, used for tasks other than baking. For example, on cold, wet days, with the oven adjusted to be warm rather than hot, the door might be opened, and someone sit on a chair by the oven door and stick their feet, shoes and all, in the oven to dry and warm them. Baby chickens literally do not know to come in out of the rain, and in damp, cold weather can easily become chilled and die. When they did get wet and cold, one way to save them was to put them in a box and dry them out in a warm oven. We can well remember that the odor associated with either of these operations was not very pleasant.

In addition to the usual collection of skillets and roasting pans to be found about the kitchen, a teakettle was usually kept on a burner so that a supply of hot water for use in cooking or for washing hands was always available. Also handily placed near the stove was a handle for picking up stove lids, a crank for shaking the fire grate so that the ashes would drop from the firebox down to the ash hopper, and a poker for stirring the fire. The skillets were either cast iron or sheet iron. The roasting pans were generally of enameled iron or cast iron. A utensil somewhat akin to the roasting pan was the Dutch oven, a large pot used for braising and stewing, generally of cast iron, with a tight-fitting lid. (The Dutch oven one of us grew up with had a lid with a lip around it so that when used with an open fire, coals could be put on the top for more even cooking when the oven was being used for baking.) Saucepans and pie pans were generally of sheet iron, but aluminum was available. Coffee pots were mostly made of enameled iron, but teakettles were generally of aluminum or cast iron.

Entering into the twentieth century there were a few log cabins or dugouts to be found, and they normally had dirt floors, which would of course, be virtually wear proof. More conventional houses had wood floors, often covered with linoleum, which was made of a layer of oxidized linseed oil, gums, filler and pigment bonded to a base of burlap or felt. The kitchen floor, particularly around the kitchen table and stove, was subject to much wear, and when the linoleum became worn enough to be unsightly, it was sometimes painted, often in some sort of pleasing pattern.

The kitchen table, where most meals were served, was usually covered with oilcloth, which was cloth with a thin paint-like layer to add color and make the cloth waterproof. (Such tablecloths are still to be found in many restaurants.) When company came, a cloth tablecloth was usually substituted for oilcloth, and if there were a separate dining room table, it would almost always have a cloth tablecloth.

Farm family and visitors eating Sunday dinner. There were no children in this household, but had there been, they would normally also have been at the same table. However, when there were large family gatherings, e.g. a Christmas dinner, and many children, they would often sit at one or more small separate tables. (As one of us did, along with his cousins, at his grandmother's house.)

V WATER

For those used to the seemingly unlimited quantities of high-quality water available for drinking or for washing by the mere turning of a tap, it is probably difficult to imagine life where drinking water was at a premium and water for such things as bathing was rare indeed. However, in the early part of the twentieth century, houses in rural areas and small towns seldom had running water, and as a consequence, no indoor plumbing. Even if there were water, newly established, and often short-lived towns, particularly in the dryer regions of the country, seldom had any municipal sewage system.

When there was no municipal water supply, a common alternative was a water well, i.e. a hole dug or drilled down into the ground deep enough to tap underground water. Most well digging was entirely by hand using a spade and pick, with help perhaps from an occasional stick of dynamite when digging through rock. In the early stage of digging, the dirt could be thrown up out of the hole, but eventually the well got too deep. Then the dirt was usually hauled to the surface by hand in a bucket tied to the end of a rope. This required an extra person, but one well digger dispensed with the helper and used a carefully trained old mule hitched to the end of the rope. So great was this man's faith in the mule that he even depended on the mule to haul him up out of the well after lighting the fuse to a charge of dynamite!

When a very deep well was required to reach water, drilled wells were sometimes used. Unlike dug

Nineteen twenties small town water supply tank. Such towns often had no facilities for treating or pumping water and depended on a larger nearby town to fill tanks such as this one from a pipeline to their system.

One of us, along with little brother, mother, and the family dog, in front of a recently dug water well in Oklahoma in the early 1930s. A brick enclosure has been built around the top of the well, but as yet no permanent support for the pulley, rope, and bucket used to draw (pull) up water from the well has been added. The well had to be dug mostly through sandstone, and some of the removed rock can be seen in the foreground.

wells, which might be from three to five feet in diameter, these wells were only a few inches in diameter and unless a pump was used, required a special "bucket" about four inches in diameter and four or five feet long for drawing up the water. These wells usually had a casing of pipe that extended several feet below the surface as well as one or two feet above the surface to both prevent the sloughing of material from the walls and to eliminate the possibility of surface water from entering the well. In the twentieth century, probably all such wells were drilled by either steam or gasoline engine powered machinery, but before that, horses were used for power.

Dug wells had walls (preferably of brick or rock) that extended from two or three feet above ground down for a few feet below ground level. These walls not only minimized the likelihood of cave-ins, but also helped divert surface water runoff (a source of possible contamination and thus a health hazard) during rains from entering the well. In places where rock or brick was at a premium and large trees available, trunk sections were sometimes hollowed out and used as a combination casing and above ground enclosure. Some of those made of cypress have survived for over a hundred years and can occasionally still be seen. Many wells, however, had only a board box built around them, and without constant attention, quickly decayed. That aspect in fact can cause quite a hazard when wandering about old house sites. The well covering may have rotted away, so there is nothing left to keep the unwary explorer from falling in. The old-timers had an absolute abhorrence of ever filling in a well as they abandoned it. It was not the work of filling to which they objected. It was the remembrance of how much work went into digging through twenty feet of

A water well being drilled in Kansas by a horse-
powered drilling machine. Photograph courtesy
the Kansas State Historical Society. In the
twentieth century, probably all such wells were
drilled by either steam or gasoline engine
powered machinery, but before that, horses were
used for power. The method of coupling the
horse(s) to the drill was by means of a
"horsepower." Power was transmitted from the
horsepower to the drill by a driveshaft (tumbling
rod) which ran close enough to the ground for a
horse to step over it each time it came around.
Once outside the path, the shaft could be raised
up from the ground.

Abandoned drilled water well casing sticking up above the ground and the frame for the pulley used when pulling the water bucket up from the water. East Central Oklahoma. (1980)

solid rock by hand, and the thought that someone else might need the water. The result is that old wells may have been covered with boards, pieces of sheet iron roofing, or brush, years ago when the original owner left, but by now have nothing protecting them.

While the time-honored way of getting water from a well is with a bucket on the end of a rope, water pumps have actually been in existence for a long time. The most common means of powering a water pump was by hand, but in regions with lots of wind, e.g. the high plains of Texas, windmills were widely used. Also, by the mid-1920s, pump jacks driven by small one-cylinder gasoline engines were occasionally to be found.

Cisterns were like wells except that they were generally relatively shallow and did not tap into an underground source of water. The choice between a cistern and a well generally depended on the local rainfall and how deep a well had to be dug (or drilled) to reach potable water. The latter could sometimes be a real problem since well water could be so laden with minerals as to be unusable. Water for cisterns was normally collected from the house roof, and since between rains considerable dust could collect on the roof, there was provision to divert the first water, which might be pretty muddy, away from the cistern. Cistern walls were generally plastered with concrete to keep the stored water from seeping into the ground and to keep dirt cistern walls from dissolving and contributing to the general water muddiness. (Despite these precautions, the dirt that collected in the bottom of cisterns had to be periodically removed.) In the event of a drought, which was not uncommon in the Southwest, water could be bought and delivered to the cistern by a water wagon. That water, in

This windmill was in a pasture near Twitty, Texas in 1981. By that time most rural household water was either pumped with electric power or else obtained from a Rural Water Cooperative. Windmills are still used to pump water for cattle in remote pastures.

principle, came from a nearby town large enough to have a municipal water supply.

Even when there was no city water system, with a well or cistern, there might be a windmill and a water storage tank placed on a tower high enough to provide running water. There were, however, alternatives. For example, one set of grandparents, who lived in a very small town, had a lot that ran partway up a hill. On the side of that hill, they built a pond to collect water that was then piped to the house and used to flush commodes. Under the house there was a cistern connected to a pitcher pump mounted on the kitchen sink so drinkable water was available in the kitchen.

Though there were wells or cistern at most houses, there was still often a chronic shortage of water and water usage might be severely limited. In the case of the mother who spent some of her childhood in a small Oklahoma boomtown living with one of her older brothers and his family, one partially filled tub of water was all that was allocated for the entire family's weekend baths. Bathtubs as we know them were virtually unheard of and baths were usually taken in a washtub. In that household, the protocol was that the sister-in-law bathed first, then her daughter, then Mother, then her brother. Such a procedure was not confined to that household's generation however. A contemporary acquaintance of ours who grew up in West Texas said they too all took a bath in the same tub of water but the order he described was a bit different. His turn was last, after his father's, and he said the water was a bit scummy by then.

When away from convenient water sources, travelers and rural field workers had the problem of providing themselves drinking water, and hopefully with *cool* drinking water. The field workers would usually take along a fruit jar of water, and since evaporative cooling was the only kind of cooling available when there was no ice, they would wrap the jar with some coarse cloth such as a gunnysack and keep the cloth damp. Working on the same principle, there were bags of tightly woven fabric that would hold water, but still allow a little to seep out and evaporate. These could be hung on a tree limb in a shady spot, or when traveling, on the front bumper of an automobile so that the automobile's motion would enhance evaporation and thus provide more cooling. At first thought, it might seem that such a water bag would also be great for hooking over a saddle horn, but that idea wasn't so good since the small amount of water that seeped out was bad for the leather of the saddle.

VI HOME MEDICAL REMEDIES

While medical treatments were reasonably well developed by the beginning of the twentieth century, many people, both rural and urban, continued to rely mostly on home treatment until well after the Great Depression of the 1930s. There were several reasons for this. For those who lived in the country, transportation to medical help continued to be a problem. Until the 1940s, financial problems for both rural and urban inhabitants were a major deterrent to seeking anything but the most urgent medical help. Finally, for centuries, people had primarily depended on simple home remedies and their acceptance of "new fangled" ideas was slow. One of us still remembers his father's objections in the 1930s to grade school vaccination requirements. However, along with the gradual acceptance of more doctor and hospital services, the number of home remedies also increased. For example, a 1930s grade school agriculture book (6) listed the following as medical supplies that every household should have:

1 oz.	Aromatic spirits of ammonia
1 oz.	Argyrol, 2%
1 oz.	Carbolic acid
1/4 oz.	Oil of cloves
4 oz.	Olive oil
1/2 oz.	Tincture of iodine
2 oz.	Solution of iron perchloride
4 oz.	Lime water (solution of calcium hydroxide)
4 oz.	Epsom salts (magnesium sulphate)
2 oz.	Boric acid
2 oz.	carbolated Vaseline
1 roll	adhesive tape

2 oz.   absorbent cotton
4 rolls   gauze bandages
1 pkg.   sterilized gauze
4 ea.   wood splints, three or four sizes

What was actually found and ordinarily used differed widely from that list. Some households depended mostly on sassafras tea. Others had an assortment that fitted the ailments of their particular family or was based on what was likely to occur in their locality. In places where malaria was prevalent, quinine would be stocked. Other areas not bothered by malaria but infested with snakes and scorpions might have a different set of medicines available. The early 1900s Sears catalogs listed a bewildering number of "medicines," both conventional and *homeopathic*, for sale. The concept of homeopathic medicines seems to have originated with the German physician Hahnemann in the late 1700s. The thought was that a drug which would create symptoms in a healthy person of a particular disease could be used to treat that disease in a sick person (15). Looking at the old catalogs, there seemed to have been no shortage of appropriate drugs since one could get little individual vials containing a specific cure for one of many sicknesses. Some of these sicknesses were rheumatism, fever and ague, piles, weak eyes, whooping cough, asthma, worms, colic, croup, earache, dropsy, sore throat, kidney disease, and epilepsy. Neither of us ever heard of the homeopathic approach when we were growing up and suspect that while it may have been faddish at the beginning of the twentieth century and again in the 1990s, it may have not been so popular in the 1920s and 30s.

Some of the non-homeopathic items listed in the old catalogs were:

Cathartic Pills
Carter's Little Liver Pills
Dr. Hammond's Nerve and Brain Pills
Dr. M. Bain's Famous Blood Pills
Reliable Worm Syrup
Reliable Worm Cakes
Blackberry Balsam
German Herb Laxative Tea
Boracetine (alternative to Listerine)
Castor Oil
Olive Oil
Camphor
Arnica
Turpentine
Glycerin
Vaseline
Carbolized Petroleum Jelly
Carbolic Acid
Ammonia
Quinine
Witch Hazel

These same catalogs also listed forceps (much like pliers) for pulling teeth, but the fine print suggested that they were primarily for pulling baby teeth that were about to fall out anyway. However, the use of forceps was probably more humane than the procedure of tying one end of a string around the tooth and the other end around the doorknob of an open door and then slamming the door! Many of the medicines listed, both homeopathic and non-homeopathic, are still used, but there were also many that certainly would not now pass the scrutiny of the FDA (Federal Drug Administration). Actually, there were few medical regulatory laws in the first part of the twentieth century and some quite wild doctor's advertisements were to be seen. For example, in a 1900 Dallas, Texas newspaper, one doctor advertised using electricity for the curing of various ailments, and at least two had solvents that would absolutely cure stricture. When radios became prevalent, there was also a doctor who used a very powerful radio station located just over the border in Mexico to advertise various wonderful elixirs.

For the common occurrence of simple toothache, a dab of laudanum on the offending tooth was an accepted remedy when a dentist was not likely to be seen for months. Laudanum was a preparation containing opium and in those days could be openly purchased in any drug store. Typically, a grass stem (used instead of a toothpick because it was cheap and available) was dipped in the laudanum solution and touched to the offending spot. Alternatively, for those who lived where they grew, a twig from a toothache tree (Hercules Club tree) (16) could be chewed. A 1916 home doctor book also lists oil of cloves, creosote, chloroform, and Jamaican ginger as other possible treatments (17). Oil of cloves is distilled from clove stems and has been used in germicides, perfumes, and as a local anesthetic for toothache. The clove itself is the reddish-brown flower bud of a tropical evergreen tree that was apparently originally confined to Indonesia. Ginger is a perennial plant native to Southeastern Asia whose rhizomes are used as spice and as a medicine. Through the centuries it has been transplanted to other warm climates, among them Jamaica, where it has been a major crop.

It might also be mentioned that dentists of the day were not without their idiosyncrasies. There was, for example the frail old dentist, who, after struggling and not succeeding in pulling a tooth, finally took a small mallet, drove the tooth back down into its socket, and announced that the tooth shouldn't come out at that time anyway because the phase of the moon was wrong. He was not a bad dentist though, and one of us, who has fillings in just about all of his teeth and has had most of the fillings replaced several times, still has an original silver filling put in by that old dentist about 1935 using a foot-treadle operated drill. In defense of the dentist's belief in the importance of the proper phase of the moon, it should be remembered that during the early part of the twentieth century, planting of crops was still often done according to the phase of the moon. The general idea was that things that grew underground (like potatoes) should be planted in the dark of the moon and things like corn that grew above ground should be planted in the light of the moon. Various veterinarian procedures were also sometimes scheduled according to the moon, particularly those like cow dehorning that might involve a lot of bleeding. The time of the phases could of course be predicted, and was tabulated and available in the Farmers Almanac.

Brushing of one's teeth has long been recognized as a good thing, but sometimes a toothbrush would not be available, in which case a short section of a small green branch could be cut from a tree, an end chewed well, and then the section used as a toothbrush. An acquaintance recalls that his grandmother, who lived in Louisiana, used such a brush and that the branch had to be a bit larger in diameter than the stick in a sucker and more importantly,

1920s vintage foot-treadle-operated dental drill. By the late 1930s, a small electric motor was used instead of the foot-treadle to power the drill. By the end of the twentieth century, a small, lightweight, high-speed air motor attached directly to the drill had replaced the electric motor and belt drive. Photograph courtesy Dr. William H. Otter, Jr.

the branch had to be from a tree of the right species! Unfortunately, he cannot recall what kind of a tree it was. (Geyata Ajilvasgi, in her 1984 book *Wildflowers of Texas* mentions the use of the root of the Plains Wild Indigo as a toothbrush.) For toothpaste, baking soda (not to be confused with baking *powder*), sometimes with a pinch of salt added, was common. Baking soda is 100% sodium bicarbonate, while baking powder has additional components such as cornstarch, sodium aluminum sulfate, and calcium phosphate. (Occasionally a mouth washing with soap was administered to a child, but that was to discourage the use of cuss words rather than to prevent tooth cavities.) It was also reported that during our fathers' generation, young men would sometimes take a mouthful of sand and water and swish it about in their mouth before going to a sociable. That way they would have a nice shiny white-tooth smile for the young ladies.

Tooth-deadening was not the only use for over-the-counter opium-containing drugs. Paregoric, "a camphorated tincture of opium" was used to soothe babies' stomachs. The only difference being that in 1900 it was available without a prescription.

Rattlesnakes, or if one lived in a creek bottom, water moccasins, were always of concern, and one still hears of keeping a bottle of liquor handy as "snake bite medicine." While our assumption has always been that a swig of whisky would make it easier to bear the pain but actually provides no medicinal benefit, our 1916 doctor book (1925 edition) says the patient needs stimulation, and to provide alcohol or ammonia. An acquaintance knew a man who said he had been bitten several times by water moccasins and always just spit a mouthful of tobacco juice on the bite and rubbed it in. Since there is no medical evidence that nicotine will help a snake bite, one is left with the thought that either the guy was lying through his teeth or else (much more likely) he had been bitten by harmless water snakes. Livestock might also be bitten by poisonous snakes, and a 1938 blacksmithing and horseshoeing book by J. G. Holstrom (18) says that if that happens to a horse, first give him one-half teaspoon of hartshorn, a pint of whisky, and a half-pint of warm water. Hartshorn at one time meant shavings from a horn of a hart (a kind of deer). By the early twentieth century, spirits of hartshorn meant an aqueous solution of ammonia, and salt of hartshorn was an impure ammonium carbonate. By the late 1930s, "salt of" had been dropped and hartshorn generally meant ammonium carbonate. Observe that, since hartshorn provides ammonia, Holstrom's treatment for horse snakebite parallels that given in the 1916 doctor book for the snakebite of people.

The sting of a scorpion was, while painful, not life-threatening if one could, according to popular belief, quickly dab on some bluing to prevent lockjaw. (Those who have been stung by both scorpions and bumblebees claim a bumblebee sting actually hurts more.) Bluing is a blue dye, with no known medicinal properties, put in the rinse water in very dilute quantities before the days of bleach to counteract the yellowing of cotton goods generally observed after washing. The yellowing was mainly caused by the soaps that were then available. Remember that this was before the age of detergents when very harsh soaps were the standard.

Lockjaw is a form of tetanus and now seldom encountered because of the common use of tetanus shots. In those days people used to sometimes take their bedding outside and leave it in the sun to "air out." One day an aunt forgot to bring a mattress that had been left out on the cellar door to sun back in the house before dark. When it was time to go to bed she remembered, and the mattress was brought in. However, since it was dark no one noticed the batch of scorpions that had collected on it. When the aunt and uncle went to bed, they of course got multiple scorpion stings. They did not use any bluing and did not get lockjaw, but Uncle had an extensive vocabulary, which he certainly used that night and perhaps the blue of the air warded off the lockjaw! Actually, since none of us ever saw anyone with lockjaw but did see plenty of scorpions, the preventative power of bluing seems sort of like the medallion the guy wore around his neck to ward off elephants. When ask if it really worked, he answered, "Well, you don't see any elephants around do you?"

Since insect bites or stings were common, there were naturally many home remedies. For example, applying spirit of camphor, or a paste made of snuff and water, or a paste made of baking soda and water, or just plain vinegar to the afflicted area were all reputed to ease the pain. Both coal oil and turpentine were painful when dabbed on cuts and abrasions and were thus highly favored for the prevention of infection. Coal oil was most used because it was cheaper and always available since it was used in coal oil lamps. (One of us did all of his high school studying by coal oil light.) A paste made of coal oil and a teaspoon of sugar was an accepted spring tonic although why the vapor from the coal oil didn't get into the lungs and cause pneumonia is a mystery. Coal oil (kerosene) is a light, nearly colorless liquid that is a major constituent of petroleum. Coal oil began replacing whale oil in the mid-1800s as a fuel for lamps and was used for that purpose until supplanted by electric lights. Coal oil was the major oil refinery product from the time of the first oil well (Drake's) in 1859 until the advent of the gasoline engine, and in fact, the early pictures of oil tanks being hauled by horses usually were of tanks containing coal oil for lights.

Sprains and bruises were fairly common occurrences and a variety of liniments was available. One of the more common ones was arnica, which contained an oil from the arnica plant, many varieties of which are found in North America (19). The one that seemed to have been most favored however was Arnica Montana, found in Northern Europe (8). Some other varieties are Leopard's Bane, Wolf's Bane (Monkshead), and Mountain Tobacco. Small cuts which bled a lot but were not likely to become infected (e.g. nicks from shaving with a straight razor) were often just treated with a dab of powdered alum to stop the bleeding. Alum was also used to treat small sores in the mouth (sometimes called stomach sores). Some care in the alum application was prudent since if misapplied the effect was not unlike that of biting into a green persimmon. The name *alum* is applied to several aluminum sulfates, but the most common alum is aluminum potassium sulfate, which is still used as an astringent or styptic. One treatment for inflammation was the patent medicine Antiphlogistine. It has seemingly had a long life since a mid-1940s Sears catalog says, "some physicians have been prescribing it for 40 years" and in 1999, while not available, was still listed in at least one pharmacy's computer. The label on a jar of it in existence in 1999 (but bought some years previous) called it a "medicated poultice dressing" that contained glycerin, boric acid, salicylic acid, methyl salicylate, oil of peppermint, oil of Eucalyptus and kaolin. Salicylic acid and methyl salicylate are both found in wintergreen leaves. The name antiphlogistine was apparently derived from the combination of the words anti and phlogiston, the latter referring to fire, or from the word antiphlogistic, which related to a medicine that would reduce inflammation. For inflamed eyes (not that unusual during dust bowl days), a much more gentle treatment was required. There were various store-bought eyewashes available, but it was common to just use a very dilute solution of boric acid in water. To simplify the application of eyewash, there were eyecups appropriately sized and shaped made expressly for that purpose. Eyewash was put in the cup and the open end of the cup held around the afflicted eye. When the head was tilted back, the liquid wash covered the eye. By blinking, the eye was then washed. For sties, the three Texas Panhandle sisters were treated with "Yellow Oxide Ointment." This probably contained yellow mercuric oxide (HgO), which was preferred to red mercuric oxide because of its smaller particle size.

Boils were (are) quite painful and many children, including both of us, were afflicted with them. Carbolic acid salve was a treatment used. A 1908 Sears catalog says that their Carbolic Arnica Salve was "The best in the world for burns, flesh wounds, chilblains, boils, felons, sores, ulcers, and fever blisters." Chilblains were an inflammatory swelling or sore produced by exposure of the feet or hands to cold and the felon referred to an inflammation of a finger or toe and not to a convicted villain. However, just to be on the safe side, we suppose, the same catalog also offered a boil remedy "composed mainly of calcium sulphide and which has for years been known to quickly check and clear the system from boils." By the 1940s, the Sears catalog carried neither product, but the 1940 Merck Index said that calcium sulphide had been used with <u>alleged</u> success in the treatment of boils. Lancing was the accepted treatment (not necessarily in a doctor's office, but with a needle, a straight pin, or a sharp pocketknife in our father's hand). As an adjunct, a raw potato was sometimes shredded, placed in a rag, and held in place over the boil (i.e. a potato poultice). It was commonly believed in those days that raw potato would "draw" out poison from any infection. In fact, Grandma was of the opinion that if chicken soup or a potato would not cure the problem, there was not anything wrong anyway. One testimonial to that belief was the fact that under her watchful eye, and with the application of innumerable potato poultices, all dozen or so of her grandchildren handily survived the perils of childhood! Another approach to drawing out the poison from boils was to coat them with a paste of P&G (Proctor and Gamble) laundry soap, sugar, and water. On the "Simple Home Remedies" page of the earlier mentioned 1916 doctor book, a poultice for ulcerated sores and swellings of all kinds made by mixing together one pound crushed garden carrots, one pound flour, and one-half ounce of butter was suggested. That same page also suggested using a paste of baking soda to "draw out the fire" from a burn. The use of the term "draw out the fire" in a home reference medical book in itself speaks volumes about the quality of medical treatment we experienced in the early 20th century.

Another approach to "drawing out the fire" was to use cupping, which neither of us ever heard of while

The first page of the *20th Century Family PHYSICIAN*
H. M. Lyman et al, Stanton and Van Vliet, Chicago, IL, 1916

SIMPLE HOME REMEDIES.

TONSILITIS-QUINSY.

Five per cent solution nitrate of silver; make small swab on end of pencil and gently touch throat or tonsil with the solution every 3 hours—a 12-hour cure. Only get 10 cents' worth of the solution at any drug store.

CATARRH.

Mix one drop carbolic acid in one pint warm soft water. Sniff small quantity up nostril twice a day. Each day add one drop acid, but not over 10 drops. If 6 or 7 drops acid burn nostril reduce to 1 drop and start over. Only use this treatment once in 6 months or a year. A sure cure.

STOMACH TROUBLE (Japanese Cure).

Swallow one teaspoonful of flaxseed in ½ glass of water after each meal for a week, or when having a pain in stomach. A positive cure.

DIARRHOEA.

Get 1 dozen stems and seeds from center of plantain as shown on colored medical plants opposite page 1078—boil 5 minutes. Dose of infusion: adult, 1 tablespoonful every 3 hours; child, 1 teaspoonful every 3 hours.

BURNS OF ALL KINDS.

First make thick application of baking soda to draw out the fire. Wet it and let it remain about an hour, after which remove and apply olive oil or vaseline.

PILES.

Mix 20 drops of carbolic acid with one ounce of glycerine and apply gently twice daily. At bedtime take one teaspoonful of flaxseed in water internally. This will save an operation.

BLOOD PURIFIER AND ALTERATIVE.

Mix together 2 ounces tincture of prickley ash with four ounces each of fluid extract of sarsaparilla, stillingia, burdock, and poke root. Dose: one teaspoonful three or four times daily for an adult.

SIMPLE POULTICE.

For ulcerated sores and swellings of all kinds, mix together one pound crushed garden carrots, one pound flour and one-half ounce of butter. Apply with bandage.

growing up. However, a friend who grew up in New York City in the 1920s and 30s remembers his father using that technique. Also, a brother-in-law who grew up in the Texas Panhandle said that while his family had never used it, he had heard of it being used in both East and West Texas. The idea of cupping, which has actually been practiced since Hippocrates' time (20), is to place a small vessel with reduced pressure in it on the skin of a patient to draw out poisons. Removal of the poisons would then lead to the curing of a variety of illnesses. From a group of family interviews conducted by a State University of New York anthropology class in 1993 (21), about 25% of the families recalled stories of earlier relatives having used cupping to cure such things as fever, boils, pimples, cold sores, pneumonia, colic, and flu.

The main difference from locale to locale seemed to be in the way the pressure was reduced. Our friend from New York City said that before the application of each cup to his father's chest or back (for fever reduction), a wad of cotton dipped in alcohol and then lit was stuck into the inverted cup for a few seconds. Our brother-in-law from West Texas remembers hearing about the cups being held inverted over the spout of a steaming teakettle. A man from East Texas said his mother would heat an empty soft drink bottle in boiling water; quickly wrap the bottle in a cooled towel and then place the bottle, mouth down, on bothersome skin eruptions. In other parts of the world, animal horns with the tip end cut off were placed on the skin and pressure reduced by sucking on the tip. This particular approach is not much different from what we did as children when we would briefly suck on a hurt finger. There has also been a compact nest of rubber suction cups marketed as a snakebite kit. The idea in that

Cupping glasses. These particular glasses (cups) were brought to the US from Russia many years ago. Historically, the required reduced pressure in a cup was usually produced by heating the air in the cup before application and then allowing it to cool after the cup was pressed onto the skin.

case being that the suction cup applied to the bite area would suck out, not disease causing poisons, but the snake venom.

As an alternative to nationally distributed patent medicines, many locally formulated preparations also existed. Typical of these was Flood's Flu Salve, compounded and sold by two old ladies who owned a drug store in Eastern Oklahoma. It was used much as Vicks salve is today and was so treasured by one aunt that as her family moved from Oklahoma to Illinois to Arkansas to Louisiana during World War II, she prevailed on kinfolk remaining in Oklahoma to keep her and her family supplied with the salve.

Depression, which we assume is the psychobabble term for "down in the dumps" was combated by a variety of means, depending on the personality of the afflicted person. In any event, responsibility rested with that person. One father always said he needed a good hearty laugh once a day to keep in a proper frame of mind, and by watching the antics of his three daughters, was always able to keep in pretty good spirits. The mother of the other of us said that when the going got tough, she would go far out in a pasture, sit on a rock and sing at the top of her voice. In a similar vein, one of us used to periodically leave the modern technological world and go to the old home place, saddle up a horse and ride about the pastures for at least a half-day at a time (no singing though since he couldn't, as the saying goes, carry a tune in a bucket).

One mother grew up in Wood County, West Virginia where a doctor was a several hours ride away by horse and buggy. She was the oldest girl in her family and became adept at treating illness and she evidently served as "family doctor." Her father reportedly bragged that there was no better doctor anywhere in that part of the country. Later, while raising a family in the Texas Panhandle, that early experience stood her in good stead. When one of her four children was ailing, the procedure was for us to step onto the kitchen stool and then onto the kitchen counter where she peered into ears and down our throat. If

she was ever stumped for a diagnosis, she never let on. Her remedies were usually benign. For example, Syrup Pepsin (for stomachache) was actually quite pleasant tasting. When discussing some remedies for fainting, one of the three sisters commented that she never heard of any fainting medicine since <u>they</u> were not allowed to faint. She did, however, recall the kid who, when she did not get her way, would announce that she was going to faint, and faint *really hard*.

Flaxseed tea, made by boiling flaxseed for a few minutes in water, was administered for kidney and bladder problems. After the tea was drained and only the seeds remained, they were sometimes chewed, even though they did tend to be a bit gelatinous. The 1884 Home and Farm Manual discusses flaxseed tea and says it is good for lung irritation, gout, and gravel. Gravel was a term used for small kidney stones. Unlike the simple West Texas recipe of just flaxseed and water, it added a little orange peel and sweetened the tea with honey. The 1916 doctor book made no mention of this use for flax, although it did say the ground seed were used in the preparation of poultices. However, according to the 1961 edition of Webster's unabridged International Dictionary "Flaxseed is very mucilaginous and is used as a demulcent and an emollient in inflammatory affections of the respiratory, intestinal, and urinary passages." A demulcent is a substance capable of soothing or protecting an abraded mucous membrane. An emollient is something that softens or soothes. Flax is a plant primarily cultivated for its fiber and seed. Linen is made from the fiber and linseed oil is pressed from the seed.

The remedy for chest congestion was usually a mustard plaster. A mustard plaster was made from a mixture of flour, lard, and dry mustard. Warm water was added to form a paste. The mixture was then spread on a flannel cloth, applied to the chest or back, and covered with warm towels. A mustard plaster draws blood to the area where it is applied, and if left on the skin too long, can blister. The 1928 *Scientific American Cyclopedia of Formulas* recognized this possibility, and for use directly on the face, said "Cayenne pepper mixed into a stiff paste with an equal bulk of Indian meal (cornmeal) and honey is quite as active and useful and does not blister the skin." In lieu of a separate plaster, a mustard patch, made of a paste of dry mustard and water, spread on a chest or back (making sure not to rub very much or blistering would surely occur), and covered with a damp towel was sometimes used. The mustard used was the dry powder of ground mustard seed and not the prepared kind such as that bottled by French's®, which contains not only mustard powder and water, but also vinegar, salt, wine, and numerous other ingredients and is formulated to reduce the "bite" of dry mustard powder. In those days, the prepared kind was not widely available and was not useful for making plasters anyway. The Oklahoma mother commented on how surprised she was upon finding a jar of it in the grocery store. A friend who described her childhood as having been spent in "remote areas" of Southwest Texas says dry mustard was the only kind they ever had. That is not surprising since it is (now at least) suggested that prepared mustard be kept refrigerated once opened. Mustard is any of several herbs of the genus *Brassica.* The leaves are used as greens and the seeds are ground to make dry mustard. In the seeds are two organic compounds that when water is added react to produce the counterirritant needed for a mustard plaster. A cousin thinks his family used Sloan's Liniment instead of either mustard or cayenne pepper. One of us, who was never subjected to a plaster, does remember the liniment and recalls that it was often referred to as "horse liniment," which should convey some idea of its potency. Another cousin remembers that her family used a salve she thinks was called "Mustarol." From its name, one can guess that it probably contained mustard oil and was an alternative to a mustard plaster.

Far more often, a lesser remedy was adequate. Vicks salve rubbed on the chest and covered with a warm wool cloth was used for less severe congestion, and for sore throats and stuffy noses. To this day, the smell of Vicks conjures up very pleasant memories of TLC (tender loving care). In fact, the smell of Vicks salve was so ingrained that the youngest of the three sisters recently convinced one of the other sisters that a liberal application of Vicks on her upper lip would cure her insomnia. Since it was intended as a joke, imagine the younger sister's amazement when the older sister actually did fall asleep while the Vicks fumes still hung heavily in the air! A lot more pleasant would have been the swallowing of a teaspoon of honey before going to bed, which was another suggested insomnia cure. Apple cider  vinegar combined with honey was also recommended as a cure for insomnia, as well as for arthritis. In addition, it was supposed to be good for reducing wrinkles.

A sore throat was swabbed with cotton wrapped around the tip of a stick and soaked in Mercurochrome. Mercurochrome (merbromin), also sometimes referred to as "monkey blood," was one of a series of antiseptics that combined mercury with an organic molecule (22). It was commonly swabbed on cuts and scrapes to discourage infection. Another treatment for sore throat was to gargle with a solution made of horehound candy dissolved in water. A bit of iodine might have been dumped into the mixture just for good measure. To cure a headache, brown paper soaked with vinegar was applied to the forehead. One 1880s book commented that vinegar sometimes was "used as a lotion because of its cooling properties" so perhaps in hot dry places like the Texas Panhandle it was soothing. Vinegar rubbed on sunburn was also reported to reduce the burning. Willow tree bark tea has been known for centuries (23) to have pain and fever relieving properties, so it is somewhat of a puzzle that neither of us remembers ever having seen it used for headaches or anything else. In 400 B.C., Hippocrates prescribed the bark and leaves of a willow tree to treat pain. Patients could chew on the bark or use the yellow leaves to brew tea (which no doubt was the preferred method). (The study of salicin, the active component in willow bark, led to the use of the related aspirin as a mild pain killer in 1899, although our 1916 doctor book makes no mention of its use.)

Castor oil (usually used as a laxative) was foul tasting, and was often used by the mother of the three sisters as a standard remedy. Since it was very distasteful, it was sometimes taken floating on top of a bit of fruit juice. The fruit juice, being swallowed last, would wash away some of the castor oil taste. In Navy boot camp in World War II, a standard treatment when one went to sickbay complaining of a cold and sore throat was a dose of castor oil and an iodine swab of the throat. It is not clear how much that approach helped any sickness, but it surely cut down on the trips to see the doctor.

For the three sisters, the most dreaded of all home remedies was Black Draught (a black powder or a syrup) used for stomachaches. It was sold by an uncle in his general store in Cairo, West Virginia in the 1940s and nearing the 21st century it was still available. Black draught came in a cardboard can with a tin lid. Perhaps it could have been mixed in juice or other liquid, but we got a teaspoon of it dry, drank it down with water, and the taste lingered. Black Draught was/is a very strong laxative made from senna leaves and was used either as a powder or as a liquid infusion of the leaves. The liquid infusion usually had some sort of flavoring added and was available as a syrup. Infusing means to steep in a liquid (often water) without boiling in order to extract some useful constituent. A decoction is obtained by boiling. A tincture, e.g. tincture of iodine, means, in a pharmaceutical sense, something dissolved in alcohol. Senna is a plant in the pea order and is mostly a native of the tropics. Two varieties, *Cassia acutifoli* of Egypt and *Cassia angustifolia* of India are used for their laxative properties. Castor oil is made from castor beans, which are the seeds of the castor plant, *Ricinus communis*. Castor beans are principally grown in Brazil and India. The oil is widely used in industrial applications. However, one of its constituents, ricinoleic acid, is a severe intestinal irritant, and castor oil has been used as a laxative for centuries.

Sassafras tea, made by boiling the roots or bark of the sassafras tree in water, was a widely used tonic. Our home doctor mother considered it an important preventive medicine for thinning and purifying the blood in preparation for summer. Real or imagined, it did minimize fatigue and maximize hardiness during the hot, dry Texas Panhandle summers. Unfortunately, though, as widespread as sassafras is, it does not grow in the dry, high plains of Texas. However, early each spring, the mailman would deliver a box containing a small, brown paper sack of sassafras bark from our West Virginia uncle who got it from the most sunny side of the sassafras tree. (According to the 1940 Merck Index, the bark of the *root* contains the most oil, and explains why the *root* bark was sometimes preferred). In mere minutes after the box's arrival, a pot of pink tea was brewing in a porcelain coffee pot on the stove. The first pot of tea was a beautiful, rich pink color, and with cream and sugar, it was quite tasty.

Water was continually added to the sassafras bark, and as the color and flavor faded, new pieces of bark were added. At least once a day the family sat around the kitchen table having a cup of sassafras tea and feeling the healing brew work its magic.

A real porcelain pot would have of course cracked if heated on the stove. The pot was actually enamelware but was also sometimes called "granite ware" in addition to occasionally being referred to as "porcelain." Such utensils were made of steel, coated with a thin layer a glass-like material and were used if the pot needed to be put on the stove and if the material being boiled was likely to discolor or react with metal. In addition to being constructed to withstand direct heating, coffeepots differ from teapots in the placement of the pouring spout. Coffee grounds generally settle to the bottom, so the spout is at the top, allowing the coffee to be poured off the grounds. Tea leaves tend to float on the surface of the tea so the spout is attached to the pot well below the liquid surface. In the case of brewing sassafras tea, even if the bark floated, the pieces were so large that they would not go through the holes of the coffeepot spout strainer.

Sassafras, sometimes referred to as the *ague* tree, is a member of the laurel family, native to North America and found from Maine to Iowa and south to East Texas and Florida, often in abandoned fields or pastures and usually in sandy soil. It is sometimes thought of as being a small shrub or tree, but in fact, it can grow quite large. There is (or was), for example, one 89 feet high and over 5 feet in diameter in Owensburg, KY.

The ague (sassafras) *tree* should not be confused with the ague *weed*), which is a *gentiana*, a tall slender plant having bluish flowers. Since ague is a name for malarial-like symptoms, "ague tree" suggests that sassafras was used as a cure for malaria, and indeed, one mother said that was the main reason they drank sassafras tea when she was small. Whether it actually helped is not clear, but the ague weed (no relation to the tree) does seem to be of the same family as the shrub from which quinine is extracted so in that case, perhaps there is some of the same alkaloid as is found in cinchona bark (from whence quinine is extracted). It should also perhaps be noted that, despite the various reasons given for drinking sassafras tea, a different (and the only one), mentioned in our old 1916 doctor book was as a diaphoretic (to produce perspiration).

Two cousins, whose mother came from Kansas and had not been indoctrinated into the usefulness of sassafras, did believe in a springtime tonic to "clean out the system." However, the cousins are not sure of the composition of the tonic. One thinks it was a lot of orange juice, the other believes it was a five-day regimen of nothing but green tea. It may seem strange to consider that *green* tea might have been used in the early 1930s since the current green tea and white tea popularity appears to be a twenty-first century phenomenon. However, green tea has been used in China for centuries, and in the United States was listed for sale in early 1900s Sears, Roebuck catalogs.

A "blood purifier" given on the "Simple Home Remedies" page of that same previously mentioned 1916 doctor book does not appear to be nearly as benign as orange juice, sassafras tea, or green tea. In fact, the doctor book "purifier" is probably downright dangerous even though its ingredients are all natural! Those ingredients included a tincture of prickly ash and an extract of pokeroot. Prickly ash is another name for the tickle tongue tree, which when chewed makes the tongue and lips numb, and our *Texas Roadside Flowers of Texas* book says pokeroot is very poisonous.

Then, as now, there was considerable emphasis on various herbal remedies, and the same 1916 doctor book shows pictures and lists almost a hundred herbs of supposed medicinal value. The interesting thing is that the use given then bears little resemblance to the currently suggested uses for the same herb. In addition to the herbs, some trees or shrubs were also used in various formulations as, for example, the sassafras tree already mentioned. Another tree that was favored by Indians and early North American settlers for its medicinal properties was the persimmon, although by the beginning of the twentieth century the persimmon seemed to have been valued only for its wood and taste of its fruit. An uncle dearly loved cookies made with a large percentage of persimmons in the dough, and in some locales, persimmon beer was made. Earlier, the fruit was used as a remedy for intestinal problems. The roots were boiled and the liquid used to treat diarrhea. The seeds were sometimes pulverized and used in the treatment of kidney stones.

Quinine, from the bark of the cinchona shrub, has been used for the treatment of malaria for almost 400 years and in the early twentieth century was available without prescription for home use. It could be bought either in pill form, or in bulk, along with a supply of capsules, then transferred to the capsules and swallowed as was deemed necessary. In the 1895 Montgomery Ward catalog, 100 two-grain pills cost 24 cents, while a 1908 Sears catalog had one-oz. packages of quinine powder for

39 cents. Neither of us remembers the price, but quinine was still available over the counter well into the 1930s.

Asafetida (sometimes referred to as "devil's dung") has a strong onion-like odor and is made chiefly from the rhizomes and roots of *Ferula foetida*), which is found in Turkestan, Afghanistan, and Iran. It has been used in the United States as a sedative, a constituent of laxatives, and for flatulence. A 1916 dictionary says that it was also much used as a stimulant and as an antispasmodic. The 1884 farm manual mentions its use in treating hysteria (presumably because of its sedative properties), and colic. A mid-1940s Montgomery Ward catalog offers 100 asafetida tablets for 42 cents and says they are good for cases of simple hysteria. Incidentally, that 42 cents was no great bargain since at that time a typical small town noonday restaurant meal cost 25 cents. In India and Iran, asafetida is sometimes used as a food flavoring.

Sarsaparilla (ordinarily pronounced sas'-pa-ril'-a), most remembered from the old-timey westerns as the drink of those too young to be served at a bar, is a tea made from the dried root of the *smilax medica chamisso* or roots of other plants of the *similax* genus. Simlax is found in Jamaica, Honduras, Mexico, Brazil and Guatemala. Sarsaparilla has a pleasant taste and indeed has been used primarily as a beverage flavoring. However, despite its pleasantness it has also been used as a medicine for the treatment of rheumatism and some skin disorders.

Garlic, an herb normally used in food preparation, is foul smelling enough to be considered as medicinal, and indeed was often worn in a small sack around one's neck to ward off colds. It has been suggested that since colds can more easily be spread when people (children usually) are close together, the garlic worked by being disagreeable enough to keep people separated. The separation part is certainly true as attested by an acquaintance who told how his father, disliking someone whom he had to work next to, began wearing a bag of garlic. Shortly thereafter, the other fellow requested a transfer to a different work area. As a variation, asafetida was sometimes added to the garlic.

A rather unique method of preventing the foot blisters that could develop from walking barefooted on hot West Texas sand was developed by an acquaintance who spent some of her childhood in Terlingua, Texas. (Terlingua is now a ghost town that is just to the west of Big Bend National Park and very close to the Rio Grande River.) She carried an empty syrup bucket with her so that when her feet got uncomfortably hot, she could sit down on the bucket, pick her feet up off of the ground, and let them cool off.

Then, as now, keeping medicines away from small children was a concern. One method, used by a great aunt, was to tie strings around the necks of particularly dangerous medicine bottles and hang them on the wall high above where a child could reach.

Another approach to healthiness, and an admittedly roundabout one, was to eat black-eyed peas each New Year's Day to ensure good luck throughout the New Year. That of course would automatically provide for good health. It is not clear where or when this custom originated but some sort of lentil has been eaten on New

Year's for good luck in such diverse places as the US Southwest, France, Egypt, and India. In some of the Southern states, cowpeas are used instead of black-eyed peas. Some residents of those states also were/are pretty sure that the bowl of peas should be bolstered by a serving of cooked cabbage. It should be noted that while some dictionaries list cowpeas as being synonymous with black-eyed peas, and the 1959 USDA Yearbook of Agriculture indicates that cowpeas are the same as black-eyed peas, crowder peas, or southern peas, those who eat them believe that they are quite different. In fact, a 12-31-1998 newspaper column said that black-eyed peas "taste a lot like dirt" while cowpeas have "an appealing flavor." We might not have called it preventive medicine in those days, but in addition to the New Year's Day ritual of eating black-eyed peas, there were a variety of other procedures thought to reduce the incidence of sicknesses. For example, besides the annual spring drinking of sassafras tea already mentioned, we used cloves to keep from contracting colds when we visited someone who was sick with a cold. We were told always to hold a whole clove in our mouth while visiting a sick friend.

There was also concern about keeping the house free of germs when someone was sick. One mother had an uncle with TB (tuberculosis) and his wife kept a supply of dilute (probably 5%) carbolic acid on hand for disinfecting their house and clothing. The 1884 Home and Farm Manual suggests roll-sulphur for fumigation, and a zinc sulfate solution for clothing and bedding disinfecting. It also comments that corpses should be washed with a double strength zinc sulfate solution and buried immediately. An alternative fumigation technique was to roll up some newspapers, light one end, and move the torch about the room. Care needed to be exercised so as not to burn down the house, and when the flames were within a few inches of the holding hand, the flame needed to be extinguished; otherwise one also had to worry about treating a burned hand. Actually, this procedure may not have been so farfetched. It is quite possible that the newspapers of that day contained substantial sulfur compounds (they did yellow a lot with age) and burning them was much like fumigating with burning sulfur. There was, of course, the problem of obtaining the newspapers. Unless one lived in town, whatever newspaper received on a regular basis had to be delivered by US mail and was more likely a weekly rather than a daily. (In the Southwest, the Kansas City Star was a favorite.)

One practice that probably did not do anything to cut down on the transmission of disease from family member to family member, or for that matter, from neighbor to neighbor, was the use of a common water dipper in the drinking water bucket. One neighbor always kept their water bucket hanging on the front porch in the summer with a gourd dipper so that anyone who came by could get a drink of fresh and relatively cool water. At least some recognized the fact that such a procedure was undesirable because at the grade school of one of us, the first day of class we all got a lesson in how to make a throwaway drinking cup from a sheet of tablet paper. There was of course no such thing as a drinking fountain and in that particular school the water came up by pump from a well.

On the occasions when one was sick enough to be bedridden, the time allowed for recovery, (providing one didn't need to milk the cows or cultivate the corn) tended to be longer than it is today, and some of the medical procedures themselves seemed a bit harsh. Children were not necessarily born in a hospital, particularly those of rural or small town parents, and childbirth, for example, might call for nine days of bed rest. Our old Benjamin Miller's Complete Medical Guide covers the bed rest issue in the following manner: "In fact, one of the things to settle long before you have your baby is that there will be no visitors until you have plenty of time and energy for them. How soon that will be depends on many things, but I would suggest, *no visitors for the first week at least.*" By the end of the twentieth century, however, a day or so in a hospital and three or four days with help was usually considered adequate.

We both remember that our siblings wore belly button bands from birth until the umbilical cord fell off. These were more discretely known as "infants' binders." They were generally made of a strip of flannel about five inches wide and two feet long. Incidentally, if one looks in Sears and Montgomery Ward catalogs of the late 1930s and early 40s, "bellybands" may be found listed in the indexes, but they refer to parts of horse harness. In the 1944 Montgomery Ward catalog, flannel baby belly button bands were still listed and called "pin-on abdominal binders" in the text and "baby bands" in the index. The usage of these baby bands has steadily diminished since that time. By the beginning of the twenty-first century, the bands do not appear to be used at all, and the term "belly band" now seems to be completely archaic. According to a pediatrician friend, a major reason for their disfavor was because of the number of navel infections. All such infections may not, however, have been due to the bands themselves. *Folk Medicine,* edited by Nancy Edens, mentioned people originally from Eastern Europe taping a silver dollar over the navel to reduce the chance of infection until it healed. (Our pediatrician friend also mentioned the binding of a coin over the navel, but thought it was primarily a Southern United States practice.)

One of us also still remembers the evening his six-month-old brother was held up close to a gas light in the bedroom and without any painkiller, was circumcised by our old family doctor. Also remembered is having his own tonsils removed by the same doctor while in the doctor's office with Father pouring the anesthetic (ether), and then, as soon as its effects had worn off, being taken home. Going home involved bouncing along over the dirt roads for several miles in an automobile, which by then had replaced the horses and wagon for travel to town.

VII CLOTHING

In small towns, clothing seemed to fall into two general categories. For the women there were clothes worn around the house, and those worn when going "down town" or to church. In the small West Texas town where we three sisters grew up, our mother wore a dress and hose for everyday. No one we knew ever went "bare legged." We also did not know anyone whose mother wore slacks. Dresses for wearing about the house, often called "house dresses," were generally made of percale (cotton) and were usually a floral or stripped print. Seersucker was a popular fabric for clothing in the Southwest because it was lightweight and required little or no ironing. Seersucker is a cotton fabric with permanently woven crinkle stripes in the direction of the warp produced by weaving the ground ends under ordinary tension while the crinkle ends are woven slack. Aprons that were kept hanging in the kitchen were worn over dresses to protect them while preparing meals, but at our house, were removed before eating. For young girls, pinafores (full-length aprons) were sometimes used to protect the front of dresses. Pinafores were usually very plain, but sometimes mothers would embellish them with colored bias tape or other simple decorations.

A woman's "trip down town" or "to town" meant dressing up in something nicer than a housedress but not as dressy as church clothes. "Sunday best" church clothes in our town were a better quality dress of rayon or wool, plus hat and gloves. We remember seeing a variety of styles of women's hats in the 30s and 40s. There were wide-brimmed picture hats, which one mother especially liked, and the tight fitting, narrow-brimmed cloche, which

The apron-like garment is a pinafore. This picture of one of the three sisters was taken in the early 1940s, and by then pinafore popularity was declining.

the other mother favored. There were also pillbox hats, which were flat like a cake on top, had no brim, and some had decorative fabric folded into twists or braids around the hat. The ones we remember had veils. Both mothers always wore hats to church and to special events such as weddings and funerals. (The mother who often wore a picture hat thought it was very bad manners to wear such a hat to church because it blocked the view of those sitting behind.) In the winter, black or brown shoes, purses, hats, and gloves were worn. Beginning with Easter, white or light-colored shoes, purses, hats, and gloves were worn instead.

In order to prevent the hat from blowing away in a strong wind, hatpins were often used to secure the hat. The pin went from one side of the hat, through some of the hair near the front of the head and stuck out of the hat on the other side about one-fourth inch. Depending on the style of hat being worn, the length of pin required might be from about three  to eight or more inches. For the shorter pins, the pinhead might only be a spherical piece of celluloid about one-eighth inch in diameter. The longer pins sometimes had ornate heads over an inch in diameter. Occasionally, a piece of fabric would be sewn over the pinhead to make it somewhat match the hat.

In rural areas, women often chose from not two, but three categories of clothes. The third was what they wore when working in the fields. Such clothes had to be more durable than those worn indoors and were often the same kind of heavy shirts and pants their husbands wore.

 Picture style hat.

 Cloche style hat.

Our Mothers in the 1930s wearing their preferred style hats.

In addition, in order to prevent bad sunburns, either wide-brimmed hats or sunbonnets were worn. Sunbonnets (made of cotton cloth) could be purchased, but were generally made at home, most likely from flour sacks. Many older women did not consider it fashionable to look tanned, and even in small towns many were still wearing bonnets well into the 1960s. When bending over for long periods was not required, wide-brimmed hats were usually worn. A completely different style of women's headwear was also sometimes seen. Those coverings looked and fitted much like hairnets except that they were made of cloth and were usually called *dust caps*. It is true that they were sometimes worn to keep dust out of the hair, but apparently, they were really looked on as a sort of general-purpose around-the-house head covering. One elderly lady who remembers them said they wore the dust caps to keep their heads warm, and the 1904 Sears catalog suggests that because of the tight weave of the cloth, theirs could be used to keep hair dry if one briefly stepped out into the rain.

Women often wore a tightly laced corset to help maintain a faddish small waist. To give strength to the corset, whalebone (24) stays (which were not whalebone at all, but a horn-like material found in the mouth of the baleen whale) were used. Whalebone had the advantage of being light, strong, impervious to moisture, and non-rusting. As part of the corset, there were hose supporters, which extended several inches below the main body of the corset and clamped to the hose to hold them up. The mother of one of us was eight years old when her mother died, and as a consequence, went to live with her aunt on a farm in Tennessee. She spied the aunt's corsets in a closet and admired a couple of the pretty ones trimmed

A sunbonnet, such as the one the woman on the left was wearing, protected the wearer's face from the sun and prevented getting sunburn while working in the field or garden. Many of the bonnets also provided additional protection for the back of the neck while the wearer was bending over doing such things as hoeing or picking beans. Sunbonnets were very popular during the 1920s and 30s when many women worked outside and when women's tans were not popular.

This picture was taken about 1915. Those wearing dust caps were great aunts.

with lace, baby ribbon, and bows. She decided one Sunday morning she wanted to wear a corset to church, and convinced the aunt to go on to church without her so she could "finish her chores" and then ride her horse in later. Her plan backfired when she showed up late at the church and walked down the aisle with the end of the corset hanging below her dress and  the hose supporters swishing back and forth as she walked. Her aunt tapped her on the shoulder and motioned her outside, where the aunt unceremoniously plopped her up on her horse and sent her back home.

Men usually had only two categories of clothes, one they wore to work and about the house, and the other was their going-to-town or to-church clothes. The very same clothes worn to work were not necessarily the ones worn about the house. Since the former might be dirty, itchy and smelly, a change to cleaner clothes after coming in from the fields or some other workplace was common. Farmers tended to wear shirts and denim overalls, usually blue, or sometimes blue and white striped. It should be noted that the term "overalls" has changed somewhat in meaning over the years. A 1916 unabridged dictionary defines *overalls* as loose-fitting, rough-textured trousers. During that same time, pants with a cloth bib extending up the front and held up, not by a belt but by integral suspenders coming up from the waist in the back and attaching to the top of the bib in the front, were referred to as *bib overalls*. However, as far back as either of us can remember, the bib variety was just called overalls. Men other than farmers usually wore regular pants instead of overalls. The father who worked in the oil fields and many of the fathers of our friends wore cotton khakis (pants and shirt) to work. Father wore his older khakis for every-day and the newer ones for going to town, to vote, etc. (but not to church).

Most men and boys wore a hat or cap when they were outside, but were careful always to remove them when they went inside. (Wearing a hat or cap in the house was considered very poor manners and was not tolerated.) Felt was the material used most for men's hats, but straw summer hats were common. The term "straw hat" usually brings to mind the hat often worn by farmers during the summer, but there were also dress straw hats, e.g. the Panama hat. In the 1930s aviator-style caps, complete with goggles, were much prized by grade school boys. The one of us who grew up in the country always wore a straw hat at home during the summer months but throughout the teen years usually wore a cap to high school and for "dressier" occasions. By the early 1940s, except in very cold weather, where earflaps were (and are still) used, hats became the norm. However, with the return of the World War II GIs, there was a sort of rebellion by that generation against hat-wearing unless weather conditions dictated some sort of head covering.

Since the 1920s, 30s and 40s, infant and small children's clothing does not seem to have changed so much in style as in utility. Properly clothing infants often involved buying at one time a complete set of baby paraphernalia (layette) which would include things like diapers, caps, and gowns. The most dramatic change in babies' clothing was not the discontinuance of the use of bellybands but the introduction of the disposable diaper, which when first introduced in the United States in 1950,

An uncle (a farmer) in the 1920s wearing blue denim overalls.

One of us in a typical 1930s Southwestern rural boy's summer clothes (no shoes, well-worn overalls, shirt, and straw hat).

was called a "Boater" (25). They were initially rather crude and not well accepted, but by the end of the twentieth century, most diapers were "leak-proof" as well as disposable. The leak-proof feature also eliminated the need to use wool soakers over diapers at night. Wool fabric was used for the outer layer (the soaker) because it tended to not get clammy when wet. Since wool contacting the skin causes many people to itch, a cotton diaper was used next to the skin.

Matching booties and hats were used when dressing up babies. The matched sets were sometimes store-bought and sometimes home-knitted or tatted, and both boy and girl babies wore them. Crawlers, garments for babies not yet walking, were specifically worn for their warmth. Baby bishop dresses (formal gowns for religious ceremonies) were long dresses with matching smocking, slip, bonnet, and booties. Babies and little girls wore slips for dressing-up, and some better dresses came with slips that had trim to match the dress. The youngest of the three sisters remembers that when she was four years old, after Mother dressed her with a pretty dress and matching slip for church, she decided to go outside and play. She knew she would be in trouble if she got her Sunday dress dirty, so before going out she took her dress off and wore only her slip. She remembers to this day how mightily embarrassed Mother was.

Children not yet walking, both boys and girls, wore creepers, either one-piece or two-piece with the top and bottom buttoned together. These garments ranged in design from plain everyday styles to decorative designs with lace, embroidery, and smocking for girls. (Smocking is decorative stitching used in gathering cloth as to make it hang in folds.) Smocking and embroidery were and are often used on homemade as well as store-bought baby girls' wear.

Shirley Temple fashions were very popular for girls in some areas where the family could afford them. A friend who grew up on the West Coast recalls wearing Shirley Temple dresses when dressing up for church, but they were not worn as school clothes. It was also very popular to wear the distinctive Shirley Temple pin that came with the Shirley Temple doll on your school dress. While we three sisters did not have Shirley Temple dolls, we played for hours at a time with Shirley Temple paper dolls. Our mother attempted to emulate the Shirley Temple hairstyle by rolling our hair in "rag rollers." While our hair was wet, beginning about halfway down on the cloth, she rolled the hair around a strip of cloth, which was eight or so inches long and a few inches wide, and then swung the top of the cloth down and tied the two ends together. Two of us had coarse, thick hair, and when our hair dried, we had long, springy, curls. The other sister had very thin, fine hair so Mother used a much wider cloth for rolling her hair. Otherwise her curls looked like little rat-tails.

The standard wardrobe for schoolboys in the West Texas town and the rural area where we grew up was overalls and a shirt. Rural boys generally went barefooted during the summer but with the beginning of school and of cooler weather, larger new (or usable cast-off shoes from an older brother) were in order. If one happened to have a slightly older sister instead of a brother, rather than wearing outgrown shoes, the boy might find himself wearing an outgrown girl's coat or even the sister's long stockings. A brother-in-law had to do both of those things, and we knew one person who, when quite young, occasionally had to wear his older sister's dress to school. Harassment from other children was not as severe as might be imagined since from time to time, many others might find themselves in the same predicament. Further, the big sister could usually be depended on to come in with fists flailing if the harassing became too bad.

Unfortunately, while going barefooted the feet generally tended to widen a bit, and some mothers (including mine) thought that without constraint this could cause extra wide feet when grown. Therefore, each new pair of fall shoes was deliberately chosen to be somewhat tight. This, of course, led to considerable misery for a month or so until the feet had shrunk a bit and the new shoes had stretched a little. A friend who grew up in New York City commented that they never went barefooted because of the risk of cutting their bare feet on broken glass. He did however cringe when told of the risk of snagging a little toe on a rock, stepping on a cocklebur or nail, or impaling a bare foot on a cluster of cactus needles that those of us growing up in the rural Southwest experienced.

An aunt who lived on the East Coast sent our brother a pair of nice, wool knickerbockers ("knickers," a style of short breeches, fitting loosely and gathered at the knee) that a cousin had outgrown. Brother put them on just long enough for Mother to take his picture to mail to the aunt, but he absolutely refused to wear them to school because he knew that in that little West Texas town he would have been quite a spectacle. In Oklahoma, where no one wore them either, they were called "sissy pants." However, an acquaintance who grew up in New York City does remember wearing them. Apparently, the wearing

The brother of the three sisters wearing knickerbockers in a small West Texas town had no intention of being seen in public with them. He was posing for a picture to be sent to the Eastern aunt who had given him the pants.

of knickerbockers was primarily an East Coast phenomenon, but even there, they must not have been really well liked because this same friend remembers going to a boy-scout troop meeting wearing full pants of the proper color rather than the prescribed knickerbockers, and how envious the other scouts were of those pants.

Mail order catalogs were popular for clothes shopping, especially for rural families. Practically any article of clothing available in department stores in large cities could be found in the Sears, Roebuck and Montgomery Ward catalogs. In 1895, Montgomery Ward sent out its first large, general catalog, and the first Sears, Roebuck general catalog came out in 1896. These catalogs carried not only clothing, but also everything from houses (not including labor and land) to buttons and hairpins.

Many items of clothing were homemade and a sewing machine was a standard part of the home furnishings. The mother of the three girls was a fairly gifted seamstress and she could look at a dress in a catalog or department store window and replicate it. She cut out all three dresses and managed to sew and complete all three of them at about the same time. The other of us probably had parts in more than his share of grade school plays because his mother could generally be depended upon to sew-up the required costume (often made of old feed sacks). Clothes mending was also a necessary way of life. If possible, things were repaired rather than replaced. Everything, including socks, was patched or darned. Sewing was generally taught in high school home economics classes, but correspondence school sewing classes were also available. Probably

When we were growing up, neither of us knew of any household without a sewing machine such as the one shown above. Until electricity became available in homes, the machines were powered by a foot treadle. Then, add-on electric motors became available for the existing sewing machines, and finally electric-powered machines were available directly from the factory.

(From an illustration in an early 1900s Sears, Roebuck Catalogue.)

Woman's Institute of Domestic Arts and Sciences, Inc.
SCRANTON, PENNSYLVANIA

This Certifies that *Florence Wilson Marbaugh* has been a student in the Correspondence School of _____ *Domestic Arts* _____ that she has satisfactorily completed the subjects as taught in the *Complete Dressmaking and Designing* Course, has been examined and found duly qualified in them, and is hereby awarded this

DIPLOMA

as an acknowledgment of her proficiency, and in recommendation of her acquirements.

Witness: the Signatures of the Faculty and Officers of the Woman's Institute of Domestic Arts and Sciences, Inc. Scranton, Pa. Given under the Seal of the Institute this 23d day of Sept., A.D. 1935.

Sara A. Byrne
Director of Instruction.

Ralph E. Weeks
President.

H. C. Rushmore
Secretary.

Correspondence school sewing lessons were sometimes included in the price of a sewing machine.

though, most girls learned at least the basics of sewing at home from their mothers.

Hand-sewing, then as now, required a number of different size needles, depending on the thickness of the material being sewn and the size of thread being used. When sewing leather, not normally for clothes, but for shoes or harness, much thicker needles were used, and generally, an awl was used to first make a hole through the leather. Curved needles were also available and used for special purposes such as repairing upholstery, mattresses, hats, and lampshades. Sewing machine needles were yet different, and required (and still do) a specially shaped shank to fit into the particular machine being used.

The father or a teenage boy generally did the at-home repairing of children's and men's shoes. The most common repairs were the repairing of worn-out soles and the replacing of heels. Since only the front half of a shoe sole usually wore out, only a *half-sole* was added. Such half-soles were usually of leather, but during the depression days of the 1930s, half-soles were often cut from the tread of worn-out automobile tires. Such soles wore well and were a lot less expensive than leather. Both the half-soles and new heels were attached to the shoe with nails. To support the shoe during the nailing, and to clinch the nails, the shoe was first slipped over an iron shoe **last**, which was shaped something like a foot. The last's upper surface was smooth  and relatively flat so that when a nail was driven through the shoe sole and onto the surface of the last, the end of the nail would bend over and be automatically clinched. The shoe nails were specially designed and were often called "clinch" nails. Before clinch nails were introduced, wooden shoe pegs were used.

During the first few years of the twentieth century, small buttons were used on women's high-topped shoes instead of shoelaces. In order to easily pull the button through the hole, the *buttonhook*, a small diameter metal rod a few inches long with a handle on one end and a hook on the other end was used to reach through a buttonhole and hook around the button. An older cousin remembers that in 1926, her paternal grandmother wore button-up shoes but by the time we were growing up, while both of our mothers still had hooks laying about, the button shoes themselves were gone. By then, pumps, which were low-cut but high-heeled and held on the foot only by gripping it at the heel and toe, were the fashionable design. Another popular design was the oxford that was laced or tied over the instep. One version of the oxford was the saddle oxford, which had a white toe and heel and a contrasting black or brown "saddle" going over the instep. The three sisters wore saddle oxfords to high school, some of the cousins remember wearing them to work, and at the beginning of the twenty-first century, women and girls are still wearing them. Women's dress shoes were generally constructed in a more complicated manner than men's shoes, and home repairs were ordinarily not attempted.

Clothes washing, with the help of automatic washers and dryers, is now considered time consuming, but not tiring. However, in the 1930s and before, washing, especially in rural areas, was quite a task. Most washing was done by scrubbing the clothes by hand on a rub board. In the rural areas, even if there were an adequate supply of water, getting hot water was sometimes no trivial task. A whole tub of water could be heated on the stove, but the tub of water was so heavy that no one person could safely remove it from the stove, so the water was heated, bucket at a time. Alternatively, if the weather was not too disagreeable, (freezing cold, boiling hot, or pouring down rain) a fire could be built under a big cast iron pot, the water heated, and the washing done  outside. The clothes were put in the pot of water along with some soap, then boiled and stirred with a wood stick until clean. Such an approach also largely eliminated the rub board, but it did make color fading and clothes shrinking more likely. If the family were lucky and had a mechanical wringer, wringing out the clothes was indeed relatively easy, but if wringing had to be done by hand, that could be real work.

Since there were no dryers, after wringing, the clothes were hung on either a clothesline or a nearby fence to dry. In rural areas, the lines were often just stretched between two trees. In towns, metal posts were more common, though in large cities with closely spaced multistory apartment buildings, the lines were often strung between adjacent buildings. To provide more room for lines and to keep people in the upper stories from having to carry their clothes down the stairs and outside (few elevators in those days), the lines were sometimes of rope, located near windows, and run around pulleys attached to each building. With that arrangement, someone could lean out a window, attach a piece of wash to the line, and then pull the line until another space was within reach. One of us also remembers his mother sometimes washing clothes in a small creek, which of course meant cold water, but also easier rinsing. After washing, she hung the wet clothes on nearby tree limbs to dry. The mother who lived in town used clotheslines made of heavy galvanized wire attached to metal posts since the clotheslines were also used for hanging such things as heavy rugs to be beaten or winter bed covers to sun. While hanging clothes, she used a canvas clothespin apron that had a large pocket across the bottom to hold the clothespins.Another relative used a large canvas clothespin bag hung on the line by two hooks that allowed the bag to be slid along on the clothesline. That bag had a wire hoop around the top to keep it open so that it was easy to reach in and get a clothespin.

There were several styles of clothespins available. The two most common ones were one-piece wood pins, which were round wooden dowels about four inches long with a slit cut partway along their length, and those of two pieces of wood held together with a steel spring. Neither of our mothers regularly used the single piece pins since such pins tended to split rather easily. However, an 1884 home and farm manual described a monthly treatment of boiling them for a few moments and then quickly drying that made them more flexible (26). As an aside, the three sisters played with clothespin dolls the older sister made from the solid wood pins. To  make a dress, she cut a small rectangle from scrap cloth, stitched across the top, and left enough thread on either

The three sisters' grandmother hanging diapers on an outdoor clothesline. The diapers were being held on the line by the older style clothespins, each of which was a one-piece all-wooden clip.

end to pull tightly and tie around the head of the pin. She painted a face on the head of the pin and colored the bottom tips for shoes. The boy doll clothes took a little more work but with the split clothespin, perfect fitting trouser legs could be fashioned.

Clothes dried outdoors had a nice clean smell when the air was clean, i.e. no blowing dust or lingering coal smoke, but during rainy times a lot of dirty and often soggy clothes could accumulate. In the winter, many times in the Texas Panhandle the clothes would freeze to the clothesline, and if wet clothes froze before completely drying, then the drying time might be extended for some days. Both of our mothers often hung wet clothes to dry over the backs of chairs in front of an open oven door. The father of the girls fastened hooks to clothespins so that on very cold or windy days, the girls could stay indoors, attach the clothespins to the clothes, and their mother quickly rush out and hook the pins and clothes to the clothesline. Because of these and other inconveniences, when dryers became available, most housewives welcomed them with enthusiasm.

Even before the twentieth century, there were some washers powered by such things as goat or dog treadmills but it was not until electric motors became common that practical washers were developed. Of course, electric-powered washers did not help rural areas until rural electricity became available, but before 1940, gasoline-powered machines made by Maytag made an appearance and caused many a farm wife (including the mother of one of us) to be very happy. The washday load could also be reduced by minimizing the amount of clothes to be washed, for example, by wearing things longer. People were used to the odor of sweat, and unless it was very bad, seemed not to be noticed, but people did notice dirt, and a dirty collar was not acceptable. By the 1900s, many white shirts had detachable collars and cuffs, which could be removed and washed several times before the shirt itself was considered dirty enough to need washing. Some of the collars and cuffs were even made of celluloid and could be wiped clean with a damp cloth.

Regardless of whether the clothes were shiny new or old and frayed, they were always ironed before being worn in public. Just before ironing, the clothes were lightly sprinkled with water to make it easier for the ironing to remove wrinkles. One mother kept a pan of water near the ironing board and would periodically dip a hand in the water and shake it over the item being ironed. The other mother had a small sprinkler head that fitted on a bottle of water (e.g. a soft drink bottle). Rather than sprinkling each piece after it was spread out on the ironing board, sometimes a number of items would be sprinkled and rolled up together before ironing began. While ironing today is done with electric irons complete with temperature control and automatic water spraying, the ironing done before World War II in rural areas and in small towns was mostly with stovetop-heated sadirons. Usually the irons were sold in groups of three, along with one handle. While one iron and its handle was being used for ironing, the other two could be heating on the stove. There were some irons that could be loaded with glowing coals to keep hot, and after the advent of the automobile and gasoline, some irons were heated by built-in gasoline burners.

We always thought that ironing was just for looks, but a seventh grade science book belonging to a cousin and used by her in 1926, made the point that ironing got the item hot enough to sterilize it and therefore minimized the spread of disease (27). The ironing temperature was also probably hot enough to kill head lice eggs. Head lice were so common when we were in grade school that students were periodically checked for them. Head lice were also prevalent on young adults in the early 1940s and new Navy recruits during World War II were immediately given very short haircuts.

Another problem similar to that of the lice, but which did not seem to be related to personal cleanliness but rather to sloppy housecleaning was the presence of bedbugs. Bedbug infestation was apparently fairly common in the first half of the twentieth century and in most households, the finding of bedbugs or lice was the cause of considerable embarrassment since it implied a cleaning laxness. Since it was possible for a person visiting a home infected with bedbugs to become a carrier and transfer the bugs back to their own home, children were generally not allowed to visit homes having (or suspected of having) bedbugs. Similarly, visits from anyone living in an infected home were discouraged. To control bedbugs, the 1884 Home and Farm Manual (26) recommended Paris green (also poisonous to humans) or borax. It also suggests that travelers carry a sack of borax in their suitcases and sprinkle it over and under their pillows in order to not become food for the "wretches." The 1928 *Scientific American Cyclopedia of Formulas* (7) suggests rubbing the joints of the bedstead and any cracks in the floor with a mixture of turpentine and coal oil as another way to eliminate the bugs. Liquid and powder bedbug insecticides were listed in both the Sears, Roebuck and Co. and Montgomery Ward Catalogs until at least the mid-1940s. However, as noted in W. Olkowski et al's 1991 book entitled "Common-Sense Pest Control," bedbugs are not considered a common problem today, although they were fifty years ago.

VIII SCHOOL

Despite the many job requirements of children, just about all of us of the proper age went to school for at least a few years. However, it was not uncommon for rural schools to be closed during cotton picking time so the children could help with the picking. Grade school children, both rural and city, generally walked or rode their bicycles to school unattended by a parent. Rural grade schools were located close enough to each other that an eight or ten year old could walk to school in an hour or less. The roads (none of them paved) did not necessarily go directly from the student's house to the school. Quite often, to shorten the walking distance, both of the Oklahoma brothers would cut across fields and/or pastures (being careful to steer clear of bulls, rattlesnakes, and such).

Town schools were about the same distance apart as rural schools, but the students generally had sidewalks or paved streets to walk on. Even with paved roads and sidewalks, going home from school could still sometimes be frightening. The Texas Panhandle native remembers classes being dismissed one day during a blinding Panhandle snowstorm and she and her younger sister having to feel along alley fences to find their way home. Apparently, even without a snowstorm, the weather made a lasting impression on most of us. One of our daughters says that just about all of her grade school classmates mentioned that their fathers claimed they had to walk uphill and against the wind both to and from school. Of course, it is no great stretch of the imagination to conceive of the wind changing direction between the beginning and the end of class, but it is pretty hard to imagine much of a hill in either direction when the region is characterized as "flat as a flitter."

Rural schools and many small town schools had nothing like a school cafeteria, although those schools would sometimes have small kitchens where simple meals could be prepared. Thus, children who lived too far from the school to go home for lunch generally had to take lunches with them every day. Sometimes what was packed was not particularly liked. Younger brother, while not objecting to things like fried egg sandwiches, did not like raw vegetables (items always to be found in our lunchboxes during the growing season). Mother, years later, said she would find the vegetables scattered along the path where brother tossed them out as he walked to school. Rural schooling often ended with the eighth grade so there was an eighth grade graduation ceremony with all of the pomp and proud parents seen in city high school graduations. For those who intended to continue their education past grade school, unless they lived near a town large enough to have a high school, they were faced with the very real problem of how to get to a school. In general, the student either had to live within walking distance of town or else move to town since few school buses were then being used. For example, in 1930, only about seven percent of grade and high school students were transported using public funds, and by 1940, the number had only grown to 16% (28). One of us was lucky enough to live only five miles from a town with a high school, so walking was not a big problem, but an acquaintance lived *sixty* miles from the nearest town with a high school. In her case, she and her mother spent the time she was in high school temporarily living during school days in that town. Of course, because of various financial and family constraints, that avenue was not open to most families.

Since so many students did end their formal education with the eighth grade, there was considerable emphasis in rural grade schools on agriculture, and home and personal hygiene. An agriculture textbook being used in Oklahoma elementary schools in the 1940s (6) had chapters on The Farm Home and Its Surroundings, Corn, Cotton, Marketing Farm Products, and Hazards on the Farm. A grade school science book (29) used in a very small Oklahoma boomtown school in 1927 included Chapter II, Water and Its Use; Chapter VII, Hygiene of the Home; Chapter XVII, Care of Foods Within the Home; Chapter XX, Household Wastes; and Chapter XXV, Recreational Science. To ensure that these kinds of subjects were actually taught, the Oklahoma state constitution (written in 1907) specifies in Article XIII, Sec. 7 that "The Legislature shall provide for the teaching of the elements of agriculture, horticulture, stock raising and domestic science in the common schools of the State."

Amazingly, we both had art in grade school, which as best we can remember, consisted mainly of learning to use crayons to color within the lines. The premiere crayons were Crayolas®, which provided brighter and more pleasing colors and were much less likely to soften at classroom temperatures. One father never understood these distinctions, and since Crayolas® were considerably more expensive than others, never bought them.

When a 1930s teacher wanted to hand out classroom material such as line drawings for the students to color, there were no high-speed copying machines available. The teacher either had to laboriously make individual drawings for each student, or if a hektograph were available, make one drawing using hektograph ink and then make the necessary copies on the hektograph. A cousin thinks she had more sophisticated art projects, such as drawing silhouettes on glass plates (probably panes of window glass). We also both remember making salt maps in grade school geography class. Salt maps were made by making a slurry of salt, flour, and a little water and then pouring a layer of the slurry over a map drawn on a sheet of paper. The slurry was shaped to fit within the confines of the map drawn on the paper and before the slurry dried, features such as rivers and mountains were formed in it to provide a three-dimensional look to the map.

Apparently such map-making was geography teachers' stock-in-trade because years later one of the sisters was making salt maps in a freshman college geography class. Another sister, having attended a competing college, laughed uproariously when she heard about it.

There were certainly no text books containing off-color material, and in fact the following paragraph from the foreword of a fourth grade Atlantic Reader (30) copyrighted in 1933 and used by one of us pretty well described the attitude of school administrators of that time.

The Atlantic Readers grew out of a profound conviction that there is need of fine and fresh material dealing with moral problems — of books that will deepen the sense of moral truth and inspire to noble action.

The grade school that one of us attended generally had at least one softball and bat, and a few students had gloves, but most playing was with bare hands. One of the few organized sports was basketball, and at the beginning

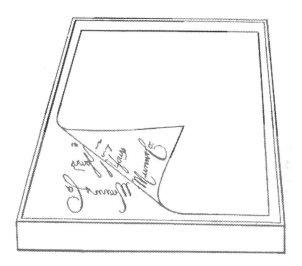

A hektograph copier consisted of a shallow metal tray a bit bigger than the sheet of paper to be copied. The tray was filled with a special gelatin and the page to be copied was written with a special hektograph ink. To use, the gelatin surface was first gently washed using cold water and a sponge. Then, the item to be copied was laid, ink side down, on the gelatin, smoothed and left a minute or so. That page was then removed and a blank sheet of paper pressed down in its place so the ink could transfer to the new sheet. Multiple copies could be made, but eventually the ink would be depleted. (Adapted from a sketch in Albert A. Hopkins, (ed.), *The Scientific American Cyclopedia of Formulas*, Scientific American Publishing Co., New York, N.Y., 1928.)

of school each fall, the boys often had to spend their recess time with hoes, cleaning the grass and weeds from the outdoor dirt basketball court. After that task was completed, rock fights in the bar ditch along the dirt road that ran along the grade school yard, and the killing of bumblebees that lived in a wild rose bush at the corner of the schoolyard were common recess activities. The things required for the bumblebee pastime besides the bees were a narrow board, plenty of manual dexterity, and good eye-hand coordination.

As a reward for the boys (but not the girls) that had not gotten in trouble during the week, they were sometimes allowed out of class a few minutes each week to sit on the school steps and clean the chalk dust from the erasers by repeatedly clapping two erasers together. Of course, if some student did not clean them, the teacher would have had to, along with her other schoolroom clean-up tasks. There was no such thing as a library in that school, and the families of the students seldom had any books at home. Once, when a classmate was asked why he did not look up the spelling of a word in his home dictionary, he commented that the only book they had at home was a Bible.

Since left-handed children generally find it much more difficult to write left-to-right than do right-handed children (e.g. they cannot see what they have just written unless they hold their left hand in some contorted fashion), it was not uncommon in the first half of the twentieth century for grade school teachers to discourage left-hand writing. Much later than that, Stanley Coren, in *The Left-Handed Syndrome* (31), still listed such discouragements as class ridicule, rapping the left hand when it was used for writing, and forcible restraining the left hand. The Oklahoma grade school where the two brothers went was very small, only one left-hand student ("lefty") is remembered, and no coercion to change is recalled. Also, Lefty showed no sign of his self-esteem being lowered because of his nickname. The three sisters' mother, as well as one of the sisters, was left-handed and while the sisters' grade school did not intentionally set out to prevent that sister from writing with her left-hand, one of the school's other practices had that effect. In order to train students to move their wrist and arm during writing, and not just wiggle their thumb and forefinger, a constraining metal "crutch" that fit over the thumb and finger was used during penmanship lessons. Since the school only had right hand crutches, the result was that the sister was forced to use her right hand during the penmanship lessons. The mother could write quite nicely left-handed and she forbad the school from attempting to change the left-hand sister's left hand writing.

The grade school teachers of the 1930s often had much less formal education than is now required. In each state there were generally several small colleges whose primary function was to prepare young high school graduates to be classroom teachers, and often only two years of college was required for a grade school teaching certificate. In fact, it was not unusual to attend college for one year, get a temporary certificate, teach the next year, then go back to school for another year and receive a permanent certificate. Even after the educational requirements were raised, teachers who had earlier received certificates were generally allowed to continue teaching.

Rural schools were often built much like frame houses, and some small towns continued to use wooden high school structures well into the twentieth century. However, by then most schools were masonry, although they were not necessarily kept in full repair. For example, the grade school that one of us went to had earlier been a high school (brick), but the town's population had dwindled until there were only enough students in the town and surrounding rural area for eight grades to barely fill two rooms. (Several grades in one room were not uncommon, with each grade occupying one or two rows of seats.) The building was two stories, but due to years of a leaky roof, the upstairs floor was so rotted that no one was allowed up the stairs. The prolonged leaking of the roof was not due to any dereliction of duty on the part of the school board. During the depression days of the 1930s, there just was not any money for repairs. In fact, there were some months when the teachers got IOUs instead of their monthly pay. Fortunately, though at a discount, the local bank would buy the IOUs, betting that the county would eventually redeem them. During that same time, it was common practice for the school board not to hire a teacher if anyone in the potential teacher's family already had a job. The school with the bad roof eventually burned, but none of the student's records were lost because the school board had "luckily" chosen that weekend to take home all of the records so they could study them. The consensus in the community was that the school building was burned to get it off the tax roll. To replace it, a small two-room wooden school was built.

Social activities at rural and small-town grade schools were primarily plays, a Christmas party, and box or pie suppers. The suppers were combination social and fund-raising events in which girls or young single women

Two-room grade school in Eastern Central Oklahoma built in the 1940s that was attended by the younger brother, and was still standing in 2001 when this picture was taken. In addition to the two classrooms for the eight elementary grades, it also had a small kitchen that was sometimes used by volunteer mothers to prepare student meals. Students now go to school in nearby towns and this building was last used for storing hay.

brought boxed sandwiches or pies that were sold by auction. The sandwich boxes or pies were, in principle, wrapped in such a manner as to allow the provider anonymity until after the item was bought. The purchaser and the original owner shared the sandwiches or pie and the proceeds went to school needs. (One uncle first met the woman who later became his wife by buying her pie at a pie supper.)

One of the school needs was supplies for the annual Christmas party, where a sack containing nuts, fruit, and candy was given to each student. At the small rural grade school that one of us attended, as a prelude to the Christmas festivities, some of the fathers would take a wagon, axes, and a crosscut saw and cut and haul a Christmas tree (probably cedar) to school. One of the tree decorations, which seems very frightening now, was little candle holders that clipped onto the branches and held small *lighted* candles! We never saw a fire, probably because the tree had just been cut a few hours before and had not dried out. Another Christmas tree decoration which was used, not at school, but in one of our households, was hand-painted sycamore tree seedballs. These balls are about the size of the more commonly used colored blown glass balls, a lot cheaper, and in our locality, a lot more available. Another homemade Christmas tree decoration (and one made by the three sisters) was rope made of popcorn strung on heavy thread. That decoration concept has so far survived for sixty or seventy more years. Now, however, the popcorn is often alternated with cranberries to add Christmas color, and was described in the December/January 2006 issue of *Birds and Blooms*.

High school experiences in the 1930s and forties were apparently much like those in the early twenty-first century except that discipline was stricter and harsher. It does, however, seem to us that school rules were more flexible and their interpretation more tempered with common sense than is common today. The teachers, in general, considered that along with teaching the conventional academic subjects, they should also ensure that their students adhered to accepted moral standards. As an example of the discipline experienced in the high school that the Oklahoma native attended, there was only one young, single, male teacher and he was closely watched by the older teachers to make sure that the female students' behavior toward him, and his behavior toward them, was above reproach. Also, smoking by everyone was prohibited on school grounds, bad language was not tolerated, and girls were not allowed to wear lipstick. The high school that the three sisters attended did allow lipstick, but their mother did not allow them to wear it, either at home or at school. Parental guidance, while in principle extending into school was, however, sometimes circumvented. For example, one of the younger of the three sisters recalls that an older sister advised her to keep a tube of lipstick and a pair of anklet socks in her high school locker so she could add lipstick and change out of the ugly long stockings that their mother made them wear to school. (This procedure, of course, also required remembering to remove the lipstick and again change socks before leaving school and going home!)

Patriotism was very evident, and at the high schools we each attended (one in Texas, one in Oklahoma), the school day started with all students reciting the Pledge of

Allegiance. In the Texas Panhandle, starting with the first grade, a picture of the current president (Franklin Roosevelt at the time) was hung in classrooms. In the Southwest, at least, there was also the rural-oriented FFA and 4-H clubs at high schools, along with the more usual Glee Clubs, Bands, etc. FFA is an acronym for Future Farmers of America and 4-H stands for Head and clearer thinking, Heart and greater loyalty, Hands, and Health. 4-H clubs were "intended to help farm boys and girls become efficient farmers and home-makers as well as useful citizens and leaders."

There were, of course, such sporting events as high school football, although some high schools in small towns had so few students that they had to play *six-man* ball. As now, there were also school-sponsored extracurricular activities such as class parties. One of the more unusual events at the high school that one mother attended in the early 1920s was HOBO DAY, during which time the girls dressed as they imagined that hobos might, and then wandered about town for the day. During that time, most towns had a hobo encampment and there was a certain envy of the carefree lifestyle of the hobo. However, it should be remembered that during the depression years, of necessity, the hobo population grew substantially and was not then looked on with envy.

In the early part of the twentieth century, as now, high school was generally completed by age eighteen, and by that age, whether having actually graduated from high school or stopped at the eighth grade, formal education, as well as serious dependence on parents was considered to be essentially over. At that age, young men began considering moving away and taking responsibility for their own wellbeing. Young unmarried women, however,

A first grade class in Pampa, Texas in the early 1940s. The picture above the blackboard on the right is of the then US president Franklin Roosevelt.

High schools sometimes allowed students a day away from school for school-approved extracurricular activities. One such activity at the high school where the mother of one of us attended in the early 1920s was *Hobo Day*. These pictures show some of them participating in that event. An Illinois Central boxcar is in the background of the picture on the left. The background of the picture on the right is some World War I artillery that was on display in the city park.

might remain at home until they married. In order to look after aging parents, occasionally an offspring (man or woman) would remain single and continue to live at home for several more years. In fact, an uncle remained single until he was in his fifties while looking after his parents, and after their death, married a similarly aged woman who had also looked after her parents. Regardless of how it was done, most people considered that if at all possible, it was their responsibility to care for elderly family members.

In the event that after high school a teenager did go on to college, some continuing parental support was generally required since part-time jobs in college towns were hard to find and scholarships were few and far between.

IX REFERENCES

(1) Jaffe, Elizabeth Dana, *Games Around the World: Marbles*, Compass Point Books, Minneapolis, MN, 2002.

(2) Ten Eyke, John E., *The Yo-Yo Book*, Workman Publishing, NY, 1998.

(3) Weston, Christine, *Afghanistan*, Charles Scribner's Sons, New York, 1962.

(4) Ditmars, Raymond L., *A Field Book of North American Snakes*, Doubleday & Company, Inc., Garden City, NY, 1949.

(5) Anon, "Airplane Dusting of Cotton Fields Proves Effective, Economical," pp 117-120, *Yearbook of Agriculture 1928*, United States Government Printing Office, 1929.

(6) McIntosh, Daniel Cob and Don Mathis Orr, *Agriculture for Elementary Schools*, American Book Company, New York, NY, 1938.

(7) Hopkins, Albert A. (editor), *The Scientific American Cyclopedia of Formulas*, Scientific American Publishing Co., New York, NY, 1928.

(8) Anon, *The Merck Index, fifth edition*, Merck & Co. Inc., Rahway, NJ, 1940.

(9) Schwitzer, M. K., *Margarine and Other Food Fats*, Interscience Publishers, New York, NY, 1956.

(10) Anon, *Sears, Roebuck and Co. Catalog,* 1902.

(11) Ukers, William H., *All About Coffee,* Second Edition, The Tea & Coffee Trade Journal Company, New York, NY, 1935.

(12) Merriam, C. Hart, "The Acorn, A Possibly Neglected Source of Food," The National Geographic, Aug., 1916.

(13) Davis, Adelle, *Let's Cook It Right,* Harcourt, Brace and Company, New York, NY, 1947.

(14) David, Elizabeth, *A Book of Mediterranean Food,* Second Edition, Macdonald & Co., London, England, 1958.

(15) Cummings, Stephen and Dana Ullman, *Everybody's Guide to Homeopathic Medicines,* Jeremy P. Tarcher, Inc., Los Angeles, CA, 1984.

(16) Moore, Dwight D., *Trees of Arkansas,* Arkansas Forestry Commission, 1960.

(17) Lyman, Henry M., Christian Fenger, H. Webster Jones and W. T. Belfield, *20th Century Family Physician,* Stanton and Van Vliet, Chicago, IL, 1916.

(18) Holmstrom, J. G., *Modern Blacksmithing and Horseshoeing,* Frederick J. Drake & Co., Chicago, IL, 1938.

(19) Barnhart, Clarence L., Editor, *The American College Dictionary,* Random House, New York, NY, 1948.

(20) Chadwick, John and W. N. Mann (translators), *The Medical Works of Hippocrates*, Blackwell Scientific Publications, Oxford, England, 1950.

(21) Edens, Nancy (ed.), *Folk Medicine*, Ahead Desktop Publishing House, Binghampton, NY, 1994.

(22) Nowak, Milton and William Singer, "Mercury Compounds," in the *Kirk-Othmer Concise Encylopedia of Chemical Technology*, Fourth Edition, John Wiley & Sons, Inc., New York, NY.

(23) Beil, Laura, "Aspirin's changing role," in The Dallas Morning News, November 17, 2002.

(24) Anon, "The Production of Whalebone" in the The National Geographic, pp. 878-885, 1908.

(25) Kane, Joseph Nathan, *Famous First Facts*, Fifth Edition, H. W. Wilson Company, New York, NY, 1997.

(26) Periam, Jonathan, *The Home and Farm Manual*, 1884 edition, reprinted by Greenwich House, distributed by Crown Publishers, Inc., New York, NY, 1984.

(27) Carpenter, Harry A. and George C. Wood, *Book II, Our Environment*, Allyn and Bacon, New York, NY, 1937.

(28) U.S. Bureau of the Census, *The Statistical History of the United States From Colonial Times to the Present*, Table H532, Basic Books, Inc., New York, NY, 1976.

(29) Caldwell, Otis W. and W. H. D. Mier, *Open Doors to Science*, Ginn and Company, Boston, MA, 1926.

(30) Condon, Randell J., *The Understanding Prince, The Atlantic Character Building Readers, Book I*, Little, Brown, and Company, Boston, MA, 1933.

(31) Coren, Stanley, *The Left-Handed Syndrome*, The Free Press, New York, NY, 1992.